I0487599

Jamaica Meltdown

Jamaica Meltdown

✦

Indigenous Financial Sector Crash 1996

Wilberne Haldane Persaud

iUniverse, Inc.

New York Lincoln Shanghai

Jamaica Meltdown
Indigenous Financial Sector Crash 1996

Copyright © 2006 by Wilberne H. Persaud

All rights reserved. No part of this book may be used or reproduced by any means, graphic, electronic, or mechanical, including photocopying, recording, taping or by any information storage retrieval system without the written permission of the publisher except in the case of brief quotations embodied in critical articles and reviews.

iUniverse books may be ordered through booksellers or by contacting:

iUniverse
2021 Pine Lake Road, Suite 100
Lincoln, NE 68512
www.iuniverse.com
1-800-Authors (1-800-288-4677)

ISBN-13: 978-0-595-38534-8 (pbk)
ISBN-13: 978-0-595-82912-5 (ebk)
ISBN-10: 0-595-38534-6 (pbk)
ISBN-10: 0-595-82912-0 (ebk)

Printed in the United States of America

To the memory of Nadine who, unknowingly taught me much.

Contents

Acknowledgments

In preparation of the material for this book, I have been assisted in various ways by many. To them, I give my sincerest heartfelt thanks while laying claim to errors as my own.

Preface

Sometime in December 1996, I cleared my pigeonhole in the Department of Economics at the University of the West Indies (UWI) Mona to find a "while you were out" note. One of our secretaries had written: "Minister of Finance called. Wants you to return urgently." I was glad. I had been trying to arrange a meeting with the Minister to discuss a matter of interest to the In-Bond Merchants Association of Jamaica. I was engaged in a consultation[1] with the association. Some of the requirements of the customs regulations were not only proving onerous without any concomitant useful or positive influence on government revenue; but were also creating an uncompetitive situation for Jamaica relative to Aruba, Curacao, and other duty-free ports in the Caribbean. In-bond merchants were still using eighteen-inch-wide, two-inch-thick ledger books in their back-room operations. Rational computerization should have required logical changes for optimal operations. I was trying to arrange a meeting to present the case for change. I thought this was the issue.

I returned his call, during which we arranged a meeting. The subject for discussion however was different from what I had expected. The Minister began by declaring that he knew I was aware of the crisis in the financial sector. He said he had to do something about it. Government was thinking of creating a resolution institution. "Would you," he enquired, "be willing to serve on the board? We are looking for competent unconnected persons." I immediately agreed and, after clearing it with the Principal and Vice Chancellor of UWI, was named a board member of the resolution company. From this vantage point, I was able to gain a unique view of the problem and process. For just a bit over six years, I became immersed in the problems and issues of the collapse of the indigenous element of the Jamaican financial services sector at a real level, as opposed to just the abstract and theoretical levels. *Jamaica Meltdown* provides an analysis of the relevant issues as well as stories of my experience.

I somehow believe that in Jamaica, there is at least one question that will not be asked about this book: "After almost ten years has elapsed, why do we need a book about Jamaica's 1996 domestic financial sector crash?" However, it is a question that, even though not asked, deserves an answer. The answer is important and should be given because of the subject matter and the context in which it is discussed. To date, there are still strong competing views about the cause or causes of the crash. Yet hardly any reference is made to well-known events in other countries, where analyses of crises and their causes provide avenues for fruitful comparative review. There seems to be a skillful intermingling of arguments that subtly exploit the partisan political divide to which the Jamaican population appears particularly susceptible—suggestions of almost any kind, once appearing to emanate from sources close to the subject's position in the political divide, are met with favourable consideration. The causes of the domestic financial sector crash thus take on unwarranted political undertones, having the effect of mystifying, rather than of clarifying, the process that led to the collapse. This kind of attitude needs to be countered. There is no better way to do that than by presenting the facts coupled with a reasoned interpretation of them.

Another circumstance that makes chronicling these events and their effects important is that normally in Jamaica, peculiar or unique knowledge encompassing any part of the prevailing political and societal processes often goes to the grave with its "keeper." This phenomenon may, for various reasons, be understandable.

In a "young" nation, legends are still being created about leaders, heroes, and others. Some may and others may not deserve the legends surrounding their sojourn on earth—both in their negative and positive aspects. Some who have been close to the seats of power are reticent to produce any accounts or journals of recollection that may be at variance with established views. Some suggest that one reason for this is that ours is still predominantly an "oral" society—ideas move more by the spoken than written word. In addition, because the society is only modestly literate, there might be little personal financial gain to be had from writing and publishing memoirs. Further, local publishing, apart from the tedium associated with the publishing enterprise everywhere, is expensive, time-consuming, and highly risky regarding profitability, and up until now, "philanthropic" support for the activity continues in a prolonged infancy. Moreover, attention to the archival process is haphazard—stories abound of "old" files, papers, and pictures being destroyed by folk associated with institutions that should perhaps view such acts as either "involuntary vandalism" or sacrilege. Yet, to create historical records, to uplift the general level of awareness and to raise the level of intellectual discourse, preservation must be encouraged.

Finally, the aphorism "those who do not learn their history are condemned to repeat it" is generally accepted—even though knowledge of history appears to be no true antidote to its repetition. Regardless of all the foregoing, events such as Jamaica's 1996 crash have had a way of "repeating" themselves throughout history. I am pessimistic in face of the human condition. Yet it is not unreasonable to believe that the more we know about these events and their geneses, perhaps the more likely will both the authorities and individuals in our comparatively fledgling corporate milieu be, to vigorously pursue antidotes.

To sum up, I have written this book to share a point of view with as wide a readership of the Jamaican population as possible, hoping its perspective will, as a minimum, prompt some to pursue a rational, analytic, nonpartisan path—at least when the matter at hand is revealing cause and effect.

I have tried to make the discussion and analysis of these events accessible, keeping the narrative as close to plain English as possible, explaining jargon, terms of art, and concepts by illustration wherever possible. I hope I have succeeded in this endeavour.

Introduction

"[I]nstances of contagion[2] within corporate conglomerates…developed out of a deliberate reliance on the financial arm of a group to raise funds in support of weaker, risky ventures. Several cases of fraud, negligence and poor decision-making pointed to holes in management control systems that escaped auditors, boards and supervisors. Thus while macroeconomic conditions may have exposed weak banks, their vulnerability was accentuated by internal management failure and a culture of quick capital gains."[3]

Bank of Jamaica's concept and description of the "culture of quick capital gains" can only be interpreted as "code," "diplomateze," for greed in the hunt for control, wealth, prestige, and power. The moguls of indigenous Jamaican finance, with little tradition either to guide them or fall back upon in their highly innovative phase, fell prey to a partly self-generated, unsustainable boom and market euphoria.

To many, the 1996 crash of Jamaica's indigenous financial services sector appeared as a bolt from the blue. Its roots, however, are not really a mystery. To trace these, a brief discussion of the historical context of the environment in which the sector developed is useful. The first commercial banks in Jamaica were created in the 1830s. They provided financial services to the British colonial sugar producing and former slave triangular trading enterprise. These first banks might qualify for the title "indigenous": they were created by British merchants and planters who either resided in Jamaica or had local sugar interests, or both. The banks' *raison d'être* was expressly to satisfy the economic, financial, and trading needs of the planter class.

Upon attainment of Jamaica's political independence in 1962, the financial services industry consisted of sixty-nine branches of six commercial banks—Barclays Bank DCO (Dominion, Colonial, and Overseas), Bank of Nova Scotia, Royal Bank of Canada, Canadian Bank of Commerce, Bank of London and Montreal, and First National City Bank (Citibank National Association).[4] Non-bank financial intermediaries also operated—seven building societies, two trust companies, sixteen insurance companies, and one hundred and ten credit unions. There were also a large number of people's cooperative banks, and government savings banks operated through post offices and agencies scattered across the island.[5] Among the wage-earning classes and the self-employed, an important but unmeasured financial intermediation process was the "partner" system.[6] Informal moneylenders also played an important role. Then, as now, building societies and credit unions were of indigenous creation and fairly long standing. On the other hand, the commercial banks and insurance companies were all branch offices of foreign institutions, which had, for the most part, established operations during Jamaica's days as a colony of Britain.

In this old regime, a head office located abroad performed the functions of prudential finance and risk-assessment oversight. With independence and the Act establishing the Bank of Jamaica, these arrangements were never disrupted. The legislation did, however, give the local central bank powers normally associated with such an institution for both issuance and control of the currency.[7] The superintendent of insurance regulated insurance services. Building societies, governed as they were by the Building Society Act of 1897, were self-regulatory. Their activities therefore did not fall within the purview of the Bank of Jamaica.

Prior to, and in the decade following independence in 1962, the existing commercial banks catered mainly to the foreign trade sector, relying on prudential requirements of the "three Cs"—character, collateral, and creditworthiness—as their criteria for lending. Their objective was not really to cater to the needs of local businesses, except those engaged in commerce and distributive trade. Local businesses that sold motorcars and products that could readily be used as collateral were also their clients. Finance to the agricultural sector and for manufacturing activity was concentrated on sugar production and export. The earliest commercial banks in the island, the Bank of Jamaica (neither the forerunner nor any relation to the current central bank—BOJ) and the Colonial Bank, both established in 1836 by English merchants with business interests in Jamaica, and the Planters Bank, established in 1839, all catered to the needs of the sugar planters—the latter name makes the objective explicit. To underscore the fact that, on occasion, banks fail, it should be noted that of these, Planters Bank was forced to liquidate in 1848 as it faced deteriorating economic conditions. The Bank of Jamaica closed its doors in 1864, absorbed by the Colonial Bank. It was the Colonial Bank that introduced bank notes into the island in 1837.

At independence, and during the first decade of independent responsibility for the country's financial sector, there was very little innovation. Government established a development bank and new approaches to agricultural finance. Perhaps the most important innovation in finance, or more specifically, capital market development, was establishment of the Jamaica Stock Exchange and incorporation of one of the foreign commercial banks locally, with concurrent listing on the stock exchange. At the end of the second decade of independence, conditions began to change. The business environment deteriorated in the wake of the initial 1973 oil shock and its spasmodic aftershocks.

The ensuing balance-of-payments problems, high rates of inflation, and programmes approved under International Monetary Fund (IMF) arrangements created conditions in which innovation in financial intermediation became essential. Barclays Bank, facing declining economic activity and profitability, indicated its intention to withdraw. Government purchased the bank and renamed it National Commercial Bank. Fifty-one percent of the shares were later sold to the public, taking the bank private. Major insurance companies were also acquired—in these cases, by Jamaican nationals in the private sector.

During the late 1970s and early 1980s, the existing financial system exhibited discernible gaps in providing financial services. The need to fill such gaps could be exploited by enterprising companies. Local entrepreneurs began considering participation on the stock exchange, fee-based money management, "deal-making," and financial intermediation in general, all woefully under-represented activities in domestic financial operations. Here were potentially exceptional profit-making activities, crying out for fulfillment in the burgeoning market economy. Existing legislation and its associated regulatory framework permitted formation of merchant banks and building societies with relative ease, indeed almost effortlessly. This period might accurately be described as being characterized by the creation of competing "stables of financial intermediation," "financial arcades," or "malls," as one's language preference should dictate.

The previously existing firewall constructed between and among banking, insurance, money management, and other financial services was jettisoned like so much useless ballast. In reality, operation of the "group,"[8] as owners, principals, and their corporate lawyers preferred to name them, literally demolished the firewall between banking and real sector activity—real estate ownership and speculation, operation of farms and other types of businesses. Invariably within a "group" there would reside a merchant bank, insurance company, commercial bank, building society, and perhaps a mutual fund or unit trust. These developments led to and coincided with strong growth in the country's financial services sector. However, the real sector was not recording commensurate growth.[9] Furthermore, the number of financial institutions was truly mushrooming. By mid-1990 Jamaica boasted eleven commercial banks, with more than 170 branches and/or agencies. There was one commercial bank branch or agency for every thirteen thousand persons—men, women, and children—in a population of barely 2.4 million (see Appendix A).

Merchant banking predominated in this period of remarkable growth. At the time, it was the Protection of Depositors Act (PDA) that governed or regulated these institutions. The Act permitted low levels of capitalization and quite mild restrictions on their scope in lending and investment. The fact that commercial banks had to maintain higher statutory reserves also enhanced the growth of merchant banks. The differential reserve requirement for commercial banks in the 1980s constrained the banks to holding 48% of their deposit liabilities as liquid assets. Just over half these holdings—approximately 25% of their customers' deposits—had to be maintained in non–interest-bearing deposits with the central bank. The commercial banks therefore made no return on fully a quarter of their deposit liabilities. These rules gave merchant banks, which faced no such restrictions, a clear liquidity ratio advantage. They engaged primarily in lease financing—an operation made attractive by tax advantages associated with lease payments. For instance, a client whose machinery or equipment had already been fully depreciated could put together with the merchant bank a sale and leaseback arrangement with as much as 80% financing. The lease payments would be treated as legitimate business expenses, effectively reducing the company's tax liability. The arrangement would of course provide working capital leveraged on the already-depreciated equipment—properly managed this was an excellent deal.

This outcome—spectacular growth of financial services in general and merchant banking in particular—was the unintended consequence of the regulatory regime. Entrepreneurs responding to these rules engaged in regulatory arbitrage that allowed them to compete with larger, long-established banks and, also, to realize synergies and scale economies in their internal group operations. Oversight and regulation by the Bank of Jamaica meant that cash reserve ratios, lending and accounting policies, were subject to central bank control. It also meant that a bank could not deal in real estate or other types of real sector commercial activity. Such rules are ubiquitous in market economies. Banks seek and indeed require complete financial information on their clients in order to lend and perform their function effectively. Operation in the real sector therefore meant they would have an unfair advantage over their own clients, against whom they would inevitably compete. With the creation of "groups," a wide variety of operations were carried on under the umbrella of one holding company. The individual companies maintained complete and proper separateness in law. *De facto*, however, independence and independent decision making among individual companies of the group was decidedly a mere fiction. The group therefore benefited from the services and conveniences of the banking entity that it controlled without, whenever it so chose, the regulatory oversight a sole entity would have had to endure.

This state of affairs was ripe with potential internal conflict. It encouraged laxity in decision making, reliance on too highly leveraged operations, and too many intragroup loan accommodations. It was a house of cards. By mid-1996, although not to common knowledge, the indigenous financial services sector had collapsed. Neither the government nor the population at large was fully aware of the situation. Indeed, perhaps through the process of self-denial, it was not yet recognized by some principals and decision makers within the sector itself. Difficulties which the Bank of Jamaica and Finance Ministry were attempting to iron out were being handled as they should have been, in confidential consultations. Bank of Jamaica had extended extremely high overdrafts to at least one of the indigenous commercial banks. Major insurance companies were unable to finalize their accounts for the Stock Exchange.

In January 1997, the Financial Sector Adjustment Company Limited—FINSAC—was formed by government to resolve the crisis that had by then become evident and finally, publicly acknowledged. The extent of the all-inclusive nature of the groups described earlier is vividly demonstrated in the fact that after FINSAC interventions, and that of its forerunner, Financial Institutions Services Ltd. (FIS), there were more than two hundred assorted entities acquired from the handful of institutions that ended their days distressed or insolvent (see Appendix C). Every deal having a mere hint of future profits was struck. Every group, without exception, was set to become real estate developer and property manager, insurance broker, fund manager, industrial activity speculator, and tourism beneficiary.

Government intervened in two stages. The first was a relatively mild one—perhaps an expression of hope that no generalized crash would occur—that of the interventions in Blaise Trust and Merchant Bank and Century National Bank. The second may be more accurately described as a wave of interventions in face of a crisis in full bloom or, rather, at full depth. The Government created FINSAC with its remit to intervene in, rehabilitate, and dispose of elements of the financial services sector that would, in the normal run of things, rapidly cave in and crash. The remit also required FINSAC to work toward creation of a more appropriate and responsive regulatory system for the country's financial services industry. The fact that the population did not immediately suffer the full burden of the financial crisis provides testimony to the effectiveness of FINSAC operations in fulfillment of its government-determined mandate. The downside was the more than $170 billion that taxpayers would ultimately have to fund in order to pay for the intervention and the resultant heavier public-debt burden. What follows is an attempt to chronicle these events and draw out lessons to be learnt.

1

Explaining Jamaica's Financial Sector Crash: Uniqueness and Similarities to Crises in General

Jamaica's financial sector crash was almost unique in one sense: it was confined to a subset of the sector, the indigenous institutions, and the phenomenon of contagion was limited solely to these groups or conglomerates. It was a contagion that erupted and spread from within, engulfing the vulnerable and malfunctioning parts of the financial system. This element of uniqueness requires no empirical research other than the most casual observation—it is clear to the naked eye. None of the foreign-controlled banking institutions suffered from the widespread default on loans, nor did they end up with non-core, non-banking projects gone belly-up. This fact makes it difficult to accept the argument advanced by some: that economic conditions, macroeconomic policy, changed banking regulations, and the policy environment in general, were responsible for the crash. Both indigenous and foreign institutions operated in the same environment. That the outcomes of their operations ended dramatically differently can only be the result of peculiarities of the institutions themselves—internal operations and associated decision making.

In the lead-up to the crash, there was a blind, unwarranted optimism evident in the behaviour of Jamaica's indigenous financial sector institutions. This was really the symptom of an underlying malaise that would break to the surface sooner rather than later. The institutions built grand head offices—quite appropriately referred to as the "edifice complex" by one of Jamaica's most successful businessmen. They converted cash and secure Treasury bills to invest, for instance, in shopping centres without prearranged leases, among other speculations. A general attitude and atmosphere of this type, often referred to as "euphoria" in the literature, always and everywhere precedes a crash. In these affairs, human beings demonstrate the herd instinct, or "me-tooism." Whereas he who cuts a fresh path does so in loneliness, perhaps even in the face of ridicule, success, or the appearance of success, brings everyone rushing in. In these affairs, however, the path is often too small for all to fit; the euphoria associated with rising prices and a credit boom masks a looming but painful reality.

One fairly recent example of euphoria and the "herd instinct" flying in the face of reason was the build-up and subsequent crash in value of the NASDAQ listings after the dot-com bubble burst. Another was, of course, the ENRON debacle of late 2001, which exemplifies what "regulatory acquiescence," or laxity of regulatory oversight, coupled with greed, inventive accounting, and outright criminal behaviour can do. The psychology of investors—as in the case of the East Asian capital flight and turmoil—demonstrates how contagion spreads as everyone rushes to the exit. While we do affirm that the Jamaican experience exhibits elements of uniqueness, there is an additional distinction between the Jamaican crisis and that of the East Asian countries. The latter crisis resulted from short-term capital outflows of footloose international funds. On the contrary, Jamaica's crisis was purely localized. To the extent that there was any movement of funds, they moved internally in a search for quality. In effect, nervous depositors moved their funds to the foreign-owned and -controlled banks in which they had more confidence. There was therefore no attendant currency crisis. This result, however, was abundantly evident in the East Asian crisis. Hausman and Arias, in discussing private short-term capital flows in the era of globalization, aptly describe the phenomenon:

> Short-term foreign capital is driven by speculative considerations based on interest rate differentials and exchange rate expectations, not on long-term considerations. Its movement is often the result of moral hazard distortions such as implicit exchange rate guarantees or the willingness of governments to bailout the banking system. It is the first to run for the exits in times of trouble and is responsible for the boom-bust cycles of the 1990s.[10]

There was no such set of circumstances as that of the East Asian case in the Jamaican situation. Speculation there was, but it resided in the nexus of Jamaica's indigenous financial system and its clients—to the extent it was permitted, or more accurately, encouraged. Once it became evident that merchant banks had a regulatory advantage over commercial banks, such institutions began to emerge and flourish. Insurance companies in the old regime were able to create groups that owned building societies, as well as merchant and commercial banks. These entities engaged in intracompany lending and borrowing within the group. Good business practice, prudential management, and sophisticated risk assessment were either abandoned or plainly did not exist, as the groups expanded too rapidly without the requisite managerial expertise. New and very small local banks, with little capital and a small customer base, paid interest on checking accounts when the much larger, established banks did not. They went on the hunt for deposits, paying higher interest rates to get them. Having garnered high-cost deposit funds, the goal of these local banks, as defined by their owners, directors, and management, explicitly became the rapid creation of a substantial loan portfolio that, in their view, could generate profits immediately. The effect of this was a general downgrading of credit quality, as they engaged in what might accurately be termed "bottom-feeding"—borrowers refused accommodation by the foreign banks were more likely to be accommodated by the indigenous new kids on the block.

Real estate holdings usually served as collateral for most of these loans. In addition, perusal of the bad loan portfolio of the banks indicates that a large proportion of these were for ventures that can, sensibly, only be described as speculative. Many loans were advanced for speculative real estate development, with no attempt whatsoever, made either to predict demand or identify and prequalify potential purchasers. Thus while high inflation—rising prices—and the boom psychology continued apace, the weakness of this modality was camouflaged, and the euphoria maintained. Attempts were made, as well, successfully for a time, to mislead bank inspectors and regulators by the process of "ever-greening" loans—a bad loan would be refinanced, or rolled over, several times during its initial term, in effect, postponing the inevitability of recognition that it had gone sour.

In general, in the search for profits and rapid capital gains, the groups attempted to grow too quickly in a period of both rising interest rates and high inflation. They were essentially responsible for investing the savings of their customers—depositors, pensioners, and the insured. They made substantial investments of other peoples' money. In particular, commercial real estate predominated, without the requisite demand forecasting. Personnel to man operations were in short supply given the rapid rate of growth of the sector. It was not uncommon for top-level managers to be newly minted MBAs, just out of university, with insignificant, if any, real world experience, and entirely lacking that healthy dose of caution which such experience often tends to build. Questionable conventions in intragroup dealings, a misreading of real sector signals in the economy and the general euphoria adverted to earlier led to bad investments, and truth be told, some "groups" engaged in what can only be described as activity not befitting their required fiduciary responsibility.

Following this period of rapid growth, intense competition, and differentiation in the financial services industry, which really built up a head of steam from the 1980s through the mid-1990s, several financial institutions began to experience difficulties that initially, some viewed as a liquidity crisis. Actually, the true condition was much worse. Jamaica was facing a classic crisis of an insolvent indigenous financial services sector—it had actually crashed. Furthermore, it became evident that not all the ills were due to rushing in for quick capital gains in a period of rising prices, or misreading of inflation and interest rate signals, improper risk assessment and unwillingness, or inability, to predict demand, or poor management. Some of the mischief was the clear result of greed and calculated attempts to achieve advantage through "improper" transactions and activities entirely devoid of fiduciary responsibility—some indeed fraudulent. The overall process, though, even if some details may be unique, does not appear as different from that of financial crises experienced elsewhere in systems that allow freedom of financial operations in a capitalistic milieu under regulatory oversight of a central bank and some form of securities oversight institution. As Morris puts it:

> The story of finance is…one of innovation, crisis, and consolidation. Industrial, commercial, or technological change calls forth an innovation—paper trade credits, private company stocks and bonds, collateralized mortgage obligations, derivative instruments. In every case, the innovation solves an immediate problem—expanding trade, financing railroads, restructuring companies, stabilizing pension portfolios—and also triggers a period of greatly increased risk and instability, until institutions catch up. The cycles are as apparent today as they were two hundred years ago. Even many of the instruments are the same.[11]

Ken Auletta, in his fascinating and vastly revealing book *Greed and Glory on Wall Street—The Fall of the House of Lehman*, discusses a similar set of phenomena as they affected one institution. Lehman Brothers had operated for one hundred and thirty-four years when it collapsed in 1984, and was purchased by Shearson/American Express. The U.S. Banking Act of 1933, the response to a weakened postdepression banking system, changed financial regulations, effectively creating a firewall between commercial and investment banking. Lehman responded in an innovative fashion—concentrating on its core investment banking. Its partners, as World War II approached...had either raised or invested its own capital to nurture such giant corporations as Gimbel Brothers, R.H. Macy, Continental Can, RCA, American, National, Trans World Airlines and Pan American World Airways, the Jewel Tea Company, B.F. Goodrich, and the Campbell Soup Company. After meeting visionaries who came to him with ideas about tubes that would transmit pictures and airplanes that would circle the planet like birds, Robert Lehman—who often told partners, 'I bet on people'—made Lehman a driving financial force behind RCA and the birth of television, TWA, Pan Am, Hertz, several Hollywood studios, and various department store and oil and rubber giants. Lehman Brothers was at the epicenter of those business forces that have shaped not just the American economy but the American culture as well....In volume, Lehman was among the top four investment banks.[12]

Lehman was actively innovative and entrepreneurial. It served as midwife to capital accumulation, technological change, and wealth creation. Auletta recounts how Lehman, in its effort to stay competitive, expanded its commercial paper and trading operations, which led to personal clashes, office politics and greed at the top levels of the firm that, in some measure, contributed to its collapse:

Commercial paper was one of several 'new products,' as Wall Street calls them, which had been gaining wide popularity since the early sixties, along with money market accounts, tax exempt bonds, bankers acceptances, among others. To serve their clients and to tap into huge brokerage fees, traditional investment banking houses began to diversify and offer these 'new products.' Lehman was no exception.[13]

Here we see the same phenomena Morris identifies as innovation, crisis, and consolidation. Activities respond to solve new problems, or to enable original, sometimes path-breaking and industry-transforming developments to take place. Undoubtedly Lehman was among the best and most respected. The partnership did, in its heyday, make great things happen. The fact that the 'new products,' or innovations in structuring financing arrangements, are so similar across the centuries is uncanny. These similarities cannot be ignored.

At the more systemic level, we need only consider the onset of the Great Depression. J. K. Galbraith, in the 1997 introduction to his classic *The Great Crash 1929*, a book that has been continuously in print from its first publication in 1955, describes what often provides the other necessary ingredient among conditions for a crash:

[T]here is…a basic and recurrent process. It comes with rising prices, whether of stocks, real estate, works of art or anything else. This increase attracts attention and buyers, which produces the further effect of even higher prices. Expectations are thus justified by the very action that sends prices up. The process continues; optimism with its market effect is the order of the day. Prices go up even more. Then, **for reasons that will endless be debated, comes the end.** The descent is always more sudden than the increase; a balloon that has been punctured does not deflate in an orderly way.[14]

Quite interestingly, and with refreshingly uncommon modesty, Galbraith accounts for the continuous publication of his book in this way:

Authors (and publishers) being as they are, the tendency is to attribute this endurance to the excellence of the work. Evidently this book has some merit, but, for worse or perhaps better, there is another reason for its durability. Each time it has been about to pass from print and the bookstores, **another speculative episode—another bubble or the ensuing misfortune—has stirred interest in the history of this, the great modern case of boom and collapse,** which led on to an unforgiving depression.[15]

Evidently, speculative episodes will remain very difficult, if not impossible, to eradicate! It seems, literally, to be part of the human condition, generated from the modalities of a market-oriented capitalistic milieu.

The cycle that leads to crash as described by Morris and Galbraith in its broadest outlines accurately reflects the path of financial crises in all financial services development from the earliest of times. It also provides a description of the basic elements of crash as occurred in Mexico, in some of the Asian tigers, and as well in Jamaica. The details will always be varied, and in some cases different, but the sequence of events appears to be indelibly writ. The only element omitted in their description of the cycle is the fact that often, in the rapidity of the innovation process, activities of a fraudulent nature almost invariably seem to slip through unnoticed for some of the period. It takes sometimes one event, or on occasion a series of events, to burst the bubble before the crisis is generally recognized and openly acknowledged.

There must however be one enabling factor in existence for a crisis to occur—the legal and regulatory framework must allow for the period of rapid innovation! Usually, it is the cracks in the framework, the "loopholes," or hitherto unforeseen gaps that can be exploited in fierce competition among institutions for advantage. Finally, inflation and inflation expectations—the price increases and "optimism" to which Galbraith refers, or euphoria, as we deem it—complete the "stage, set, and dramatis personae" for the crisis to play out. All of these were present in Jamaica from the late 1980s to mid-1990s. Curtain call came abruptly to the society, but some had a pretty good idea when opening day would be.

CRASH, CAUSE AND EFFECT: COMPETING INTERPRETATIONS

Jamaica's democracy is arranged around a vibrant two-party system that sometimes reminds one more of committed partisans dueling, rather than rival political parties—Her Majesty's Government and Loyal Opposition—in contest. In such an atmosphere, opinion is often coloured by which political party the opinion holder supports. Worse, perhaps sadly, opinions and argument are often judged by the perception of which party the purveyor is presumed or believed to support. In the popular press, government policy has been blamed for the collapse of these financial institutions. The finance Minister has been portrayed in one newspaper as having never had to meet a "pay-bill," hence ignorant about the affairs of business. He has been accused of suffering from a most egregious fault—that of arrogance. Others have suggested that the government and Minister of Finance harboured a vendetta against one of the principals of Century National Bank—Donovan Crawford—hence closure of that bank. They argue that the Peoples National Party (PNP), the party forming the government at the time, had never forgiven Mr. Crawford for bidding down the exchange rate (devaluing) of the Jamaican dollar in a U.S. dollar auction purchase from the Embassy of the United States. It is however a far cry from arrogance and lack of business acumen to embark on procedures that would require expenditure of billions of dollars for little or no return—even if it is taxpayer dollars! Yet again, many delinquent borrowers, among others, chastise government for its high interest rate policy and subsequent rapid turnaround to a low inflation model for the macro economy. The causes of the crisis, however, are straightforward and do not require conspiracy theories as explanations.

Paul Chen-Young, CEO of the Eagle Group—the first bankrupt entity acquired by FINSAC for $1.00—presents the case for the financial sector as victim of circumstances created entirely by the government's monetary and macroeconomic policy. The title of Chen-Young's piece is in itself instructive: *With All Good Intentions: The Collapse of Jamaica's Financial Sector.* Firstly, there is the appeal to objectives, ends and not means. "Intentions" of the institutions' principals and management were "all good." Secondly, no distinction is made between the indigenous and foreign-controlled entities. He suggests that:

> the economic climate that prevailed in the 1990s contributed to the downfall of the sector. Inappropriate and inconsistent monetary policy created hardships, resulting in the inability of borrowers to repay loans, inadequate returns on investments to cover funding costs, and falling values in investment portfolio and property values...Fluctuations in monetary policy and the resulting inflation, along with a 0.3 percent average annual growth rate in gross domestic product (GDP) between 1990 and 1997, created an unfavorable operating environment for business and made it difficult for them to service their debts. Ultimately, the problems spilled over into the financial sector.[16]

Chen-Young turns causation on its head. These are not problems that "spilled over into the financial sector." Rather, these elements provide the actual bedrock upon which any financial sector is built and with which it must continuously cope. Surely banking executives and risk assessment managers must consider the economic and business environment in which they, and more importantly, their clients, operate. It is indisputable in the industry that loans ought not to be approved independent of consideration of the potential borrower's ability to repay, credible cash flow projections, and evaluation of risk. Indigenous bankers seemed to be of the view that real estate collateral, even when patently illiquid and booked at inflated prices, was good cover for loan default risk. Banks never, in their assessments of borrowers and their projects, rely on collateral to repay loans. Liquidation of pledged collateral is always a last resort. Furthermore, any risk assessment procedure worth the name would in addition also include forecasts of policy positions, economic performance, and demand for the products or services which the loan proceeds are meant to fund. Chen-Young blames these conditions that, in his interpretation, can only be viewed as creeping up in the dark to create a mugging of the financial sector rather than admitting that the sector's failure to engage in prudential management, together with its "get-rich-quick mentality" (the reader may wish to substitute either "the Bank of Jamaica's 'culture of quick capital gains,'" or the plain English word, "greed"), contributed to, or perhaps mandated, the failure of inefficient businesses. Even more telling is the fact that many of these failed businesses were operations of connected parties, all functioning on the basis of Galbraith's "optimism with its market effect." It is also, as indicated earlier, particularly awkward for this view that the foreign-controlled banks did not collapse. When viral or bacterial contamination of a pond with two species of fish occurs, and only one succumbs, the only explanation for the survival of the other must be that the survivor was "putting up resistance" and had immunity—however attained.

Government's economic policy did indeed contribute to the crash, but not at all in the way Chen-Young depicts. One of the reasons for the sector's collapse was the very policies that allowed indigenous financial services to grow so fast in the first place. Divestment of financial services in the late 1980s and early 1990s to inadequately capitalized domestic entities could be viewed as the foundation of potential problems—which, to be sure, were not inevitable. But failure to foresee the problems that could derive from outmoded, inappropriate, and ineffective legislation for the new situation was unfortunately coupled with inadequate regulatory supervision. Previous to this, the overseas head offices of foreign commercial banks performed the oversight role. It must be pointed out that this oversight role, and the way it was performed—a holdover from the colonial period—tended to dictate a conservative financial climate, a climate hostile to innovation, a climate perhaps hostile even to prudential risk taking. This of course would act as a drag on economic growth and development. But it was as well a climate that, clearly, would tend to preclude a financial crisis. Once the innovative interventions of the indigenous institutions began to emerge, the historical experiences of other countries should have been seen to be important, and regulatory changes should then have become a prime part of government's policy. Tightening monetary policy to curb the credit boom and halt inflation, enacting legislation to provide more prudential arrangements after the fact simply precipitated the bubble's burst. With this in mind, review of the available evidence suggests these factors, along with a combination of several others, eventually led to collapse. As with so many other phenomena, there is a clear but not widely known history to the ultimate outcome that we explore below.

During the mid-1970s and early 1980s period of Jamaica's standby and other borrowing relationships with the IMF, liberalization of the trade and payments regime was always one of the fundamental objectives of that institution. Internationally, most certainly in the West, the influence of the Thatcher/Reagan nexus of privatization and release of market forces was ubiquitous. In Jamaica a more liberal approach to foreign trade was embraced in the 1980s, when protection of domestic industry was abandoned as inefficient and counterproductive. Shortly thereafter, privatization became a matter of policy as well as a means of raising money for government coffers—banks, hotel properties, parts of the sugar industry—were all privatized to local institutions with fragile and purely localized capital bases. These were eggs all in one local basket! This was bad policy, driven in part by ideology. Even the country's London St. James Court embassy was sold in the government's privatizing and fund-raising effort!

In addition to this, the late 1980s and early 1990s brought further changes in the policy environment. Fiat and direct controls, which had characterized the financial sector of the 1970s and early 1980s, were replaced by a more modern, stringent regulatory framework and removal of restrictions on foreign exchange transactions. Regulations would of course be supervised by the Bank of Jamaica. In part, this change was a necessary complement to embracing liberalization and attempts to foster an efficient market system. The IMF and World Bank were always in favour of "modernizing" the financial sector. This was viewed both as part of the necessary infrastructure of a market economy and a requirement for staying with modern trends elsewhere in the world.[17]

Legislation in the form of the Bank of Jamaica (Amendment) Act, 1992, the Banking Act, 1992, and the Financial Institutions Act, 1992 was enacted to give effect to the new policy thrust. Among other features, these included provisions for the management of foreign exchange and gave statutory recognition to the Department of Bank Inspection, whose task it would be to police the new, more robust regulations. They also included new provisions for licensing banks, minimum capital requirements, stronger prudential controls, and enhanced provisioning for loan losses. Finally, merchant banks and other non-bank financial intermediaries or near-banks taking deposits but not offering banking services like checking accounts—creating money in the classic sense—formerly governed by the Protection of Depositors Act (PDA), were brought into the regulatory net. The problem was that the horse had by then already bolted. Legislation was too late in coming. As discussed in our quote from Morris, rapid innovation had already occurred prior to these changes in regulation.

As Bonnick notes, "Almost as soon as the ink was dry on the 1992 legislation it was recognized that further changes were necessary."[18] However, Bonnick's commentary appears to present us with a contradiction. He argues that

> while this legislation was timely, the necessary institutional complements took longer to be developed. The supervision of insurance did not undergo strengthening paralleled with the supervision of banks.[19]

This latter situation, however, is only to be expected. Some form of mischief is identified. Legislation is created to avoid or correct it. Institutional and oversight complements must by definition follow. The speed at which this is accomplished depends on the resources available to the system at the time. When it is further noted that during the period of rapid innovation, insurance companies bought banks, while banks were creating insurance companies, and holding companies were establishing building societies and simultaneously owning commercial banks, it becomes clear that the legislation, not to mention the oversight complements, were indeed all late in coming. They had to be late in coming precisely because the existing/ongoing mischief had not, and indeed, could not yet, have been unambiguously identified in practice.

Undeniably, the changed legislative environment allowed regulatory authorities access to the evidence to definitively identify some of the more unsustainable practices of the PDA institutions. But Chen-Young[20] and others suggest that liberalization and the changed regulatory and policy environment were the major cause of the crisis. In interviews with bankers associated with the failed institutions, several lay the blame for collapse on one particular requirement of the new regime. Prior to the new legislation, commercial banks were required to make provision for non-performing, bad, or "sour" loans after a period of six months—180 days. This was changed to three months, or 90 days, in keeping with the more prudential, modern trends. Chen-Young blames this new provision for the sector's problems. In his view it had an

> adverse affect [*sic*] on the profitability of banks as illustrated by the fact that the largest domestically owned bank (National Commercial Bank) was forced to classify J$13.5 billion of its loans as non-performing. This amounted to nearly four times the bank's capital base of J$3.8 billion, and FINSAC came to the rescue by purchasing these loans as well as a J$7 billion loan due from the bank's parent, Mutual Life Insurance Company [*sic*].[21]

Given the widespread practice of ever-greening loans, this view is unsustainable. The banks were accruing interest on loans and booking profits on assets (the bad loans) on which no payments had been made for six months and which never stood a chance of ever being repaid. Although hindsight demonstrates this, simple logic would indicate it is a much better practice to recognize failure early, thus cauterizing any potential intensification in negative repercussions. But perhaps more importantly, reporting profits from interest accrued in the context of ever-greening loans seems more like fiction and deceptiveness in reporting practice than good accounting and audit standards.

One particularly significant feature Chen-Young's comment reveals but omits to highlight is the absence of proper regulatory control. How can a bank's parent company or, for that matter, any single borrower be allowed to amass loans to the tune of multiples of "the bank's capital base"? Worse, this significant contributor to the crisis—loans to connected parties—was neither regulated nor policed. One of National Commercial Bank's parents, Jamaica Mutual Life Assurance Society, was indeed allowed to have a non-performing loan equivalent to twice the bank's capital base. But this tendency was by no means unique in the system. Life of Jamaica owned Citizens Bank, Crown Eagle Life Insurance was grouped with Eagle Commercial Bank, Island Life Insurance Company and Victoria Mutual Building Society owned Island Victoria Bank. All of these banks either had large loans to their parent or associated companies to cover policy encashment in the 1990s, or were significantly exposed in large and costly real estate and other projects gone sour.

Another perhaps more insidious practice of the indigenous banks was the issuance of loans to borrowers who had previously accumulated and abandoned debt with other institutions. Bad loans to the same parties would frequently turn up on the books of more than one of the failed banks. Jamaican bank secrecy laws do not allow the sharing of readily available credit information that is standard practice in, for instance, the United States. Yet absent information sharing in the small, close-knit society that Jamaica is should not have proved to be an insurmountable barrier—indeed the closely knit nature of the business community suggests this was merely a minor impediment, which could readily be defeated by a quick phone call—it certainly could not have been an absolutely binding constraint. In other words, if loan officers wished to know, they could have. But with no hard information on the file, such officers could see themselves as protected from sanction. Additionally it was a fairly common practice for some branch bank managers to avoid the caps on their branch lending limits by arranging for a preferred customer to have several loans at different branches of a bank within the particular branch manager's limit. A common scenario would work like this: a branch manager with a lending approval limit of $10 million would arrange for a preferred customer in real estate development to borrow $30 million by approaching two of his colleague branch managers with similar $10 million limits. None of the managers would be in breach of the limit guideline, but the real estate subdivision development, at a cost of $30 million, would proceed without the scrutiny of the bank's higher-level loan approval committee. In the early stages of rising real estate prices, such schemes worked and were hugely profitable. Borrowers rushed in, and becoming a "developer" was the "in" thing. The problem was that such schemes are unsustainable in the long run. In such an atmosphere of extreme competition for business, the quick-profit/capital gain model simply provided added fuel to this hazardous practice.

Cut-throat competition was also responsible for another, perhaps predictable cause of the crisis and crash. Principals at Island Life Insurance Company, for instance, argued that some of their activities were specifically based on the need to respond to the competition. The company was viewed as losing ground. With top performing agents being enticed away, rewards had to be improved and the company's profile ramped up. All of this was done to be in lockstep with the prevailing vision. But a more systemic consequence of intense competition predisposes systems to crash. Discussing the demise of the unique and initially fabulously profitable U.S. hedge fund, Long-Term Capital Management, Richard Dunn, head of Merrill Lynch debt markets in Europe and the United Kingdom argued that "it took uncommon courage to refuse to lend, for it would have meant squandering business to the competition...it wasn't a mistake we made singly for Long-Term. The whole market was pressuring us. To suffer the organization telling you that you are losing business—it takes a tremendous amount of [courage] to stand up and say, 'I'm not going to do it'. The Street all got that collectively wrong."[22] Wall Street, the metaphor for the 'Market', gives off signals which for a time have a self-fulfilling drive. This phenomenon was endemic in the lead up to Jamaica's crisis.

Another feature having negative consequences for the indigenous financial services sector centres on the society's small size and a pervasive unwillingness to separate the "office" from the "official" and the "person" holding office. As a result, protocol and rules often fell by the wayside. Peculiarities of the indigenous financial services sector made this problem particularly acute. Saying no to a previously good, or for that matter, any, client is one of the banker's most important but difficult tasks. Foreign-controlled banks had a distant and anonymous decision maker for large loans—head office took those decisions, the local manager merely conveyed bad news with appropriate apologies. There was no confusion of "office," "official," and "person" holding that position pro tem—no embarrassment. Local owner/managers, on the other hand, appear to have found it difficult to take the hard-nosed business decisions and therefore say no to important clients who may have held either high status or office in the society.

Decisions influenced by these considerations sometimes led local banks to end up "beneficial owner" of real estate they did not want and for which they could find no buyers—properties which provided neither a return on their owners' capital nor sufficient income for their basic upkeep. One final point should be introduced here from the provinces of the historian, sociologist, and psychologist. From the days of the plantation and slavery, status in Jamaican society has been ascribed. Ascription begins at the tip-top of the pyramid with whiteness and moves downward through the various in-between shades of brown before reaching its base and blackness. The colour/class nexus is a complex fact of Jamaican and Caribbean life—as distinct from race and ethnicity in the United States—whose existence, even if waning, need not detain us. Its ramifications, however, are profound. The emerging black businessman, banker, or financial sector executive must show his arrival to a position of status, responsibility, and power by the external trappings of his/her office. This takes form in part by displays of conspicuous consumption. The "edifice complex" referred to earlier is an element and partial result of this phenomenon. How else can one explain the behaviour of the CEO who chooses to purchase a house in an upscale residential area, almost literally demolish it, and replace it with a mansion, inclusive of imported Italian marble staircase? How explain the oversize refrigerator in a "show kitchen" that is never used as such? How explain double expenditures on flooring and carpeting for a head office with no utilitarian value whatsoever?[23]

Itinerant street boys are aware of this issue of class and status, its physical trappings and ultimate economic ramifications. All one needs to do is drive a beat-up Volkswagen and stop at a busy Kingston intersection one day, and on the next, change to a well-detailed Mercedes Benz. The differential reception will be overwhelming. In the one case the boy cleaners will attack your windshield with mildly dirty soapy water and sponge, seeking "a money" or a "lunch"; in the other, they may simply look into the warm, open, non-air-conditioned interior of the VW to see if you were stupid enough to leave an unattended handbag on the seat.

Yet there is another reinforcing or collaborative perspective that may be taken toward this spate of costly conspicuous consumption. At the collapse and sale of Lehman, the director of personnel thought a way of life, books and people was being lost:

> Investment banking houses like Lehman reeked of a kind of luxury…see the forty-third floor. Impressing clients was part of the firm's history. The partners' dining room is particularly opulent. That filters down into the culture of the firm. The offices are done in a lovely wood finish. Typical of what used to be old partnerships. Partners felt independent. On the other hand, the retail houses are very highly structured and highly managed and conscious of cost control. At Shearson, their human resources [personnel] departments' desks are battleship gray, their floors are covered with linoleum, their phones are black. At Shearson, expenses are on everyone's lips.
>   Secretaries complained…"you've got to fill out a form for everything you do"…[C]omplained one exasperated secretary…"I know this is sheer snob-

bery, but the class of people is different. You're dealing with a lot of polyester here. The morale is very low."...[The] director of Lehman's dining facilities...was trained at the École Hôtellerie in Lausanne, Switzerland, and at the Cordon Bleu in Paris. To him the Lehman ambience—the...sterling silver cigarette boxes and salt-and-pepper shakers, the fresh flowers, the Impressionist paintings, the tuxedoed waiters—honored the entrepreneurs who dined there and perfumed Lehman with an air of elite **first class**...[He] worried that Shearson managers would focus on the expense, not on the purpose of the expense. In the first year and a half after the merger, those fears proved groundless.[24]

The human and social/societal element of business and corporate culture is perfectly depicted here. There is class snobbery, a catering to the need for successful entrepreneurs and high executives to be made to feel special, unique—the culture of sparing no expense. As we learn from the final sentence of the quote, Lehman employees' fears were, on this score, unfounded. The points of comparison to, and distinction from, events in Jamaica and its indigenous corporate culture, however, are those of fiduciary responsibility, prudence, and risk of other people's money and capital. Granted, at Lehman, as in Jamaica, compensation packages were generous—perhaps overly generous. The big difference though, was that at Lehman partners came to the table with their own capital and risked it. Indeed at the time of sale, they lost some of it.[25] They created an ambience for their operations that set them apart from most of the competition, and viewed these expenses as purposive. Not only were they purposive, more importantly, they were affordable from their own operations.

On the other hand, in the Jamaican situation managers' capital was often not being risked; and when it was, it was proportionately minuscule compared to that of others to whom they should have had a relationship of trust and fiduciary responsibility. Whether these expenditures could be considered purposive is highly debatable. They were clearly unaffordable—imprudent and, as it turned out, quite badly mistimed.

In light of these identifiable problems, to lay blame at the feet of the new 1992 legislation seems to be flying in the face of the readily discernable evidence. Conditions leading to the collapse were robustly developed by the time this legislation came into effect. The real and immediate result of the new legislation was to enable regulators legal access—through the books of affected institutions—to the true and exact image of a condition they had already recognized in conjecture.

With respect to the difficulties initially faced by the insurance companies, these can be traced in part to introduction in the early 1990s of new insurance products offering life insurance with an investment component. These new products—investment or lump-sum policies—allowed the insurance companies legally to function almost as deposit-taking institutions or investment houses under the guise of being paid insurance premiums. A small amount of the premiums went toward life insurance, with the major proportion being used for investment. The existing regulations effectively allowed policyholders in this scenario to be investors, receiving a variable monthly return on their investment. If they kept their policies in force for three years, their gains would go untaxed.

Prudential standards require financial management of insurance companies to maintain sufficient liquidity to meet withdrawals or surrender of existing policies by policyholders. In the competition for capital gain, however, these funds were used predominantly for investment in real estate, securities, and the stock market—for the most part entirely localized in Jamaica. With these funds tied up in long-term investments and under-performing assets, when policyholders surrendered their investment policies or made withdrawals, the companies experienced liquidity problems. They simply did not have sufficient cash. It is here that the group structure appeared to present an immediate and easy solution which, in the end, turned out to be the beginning nightmare of the soon-to-emerge full-blown crisis.

The companies borrowed funds from unconnected parties by issuing commercial paper, a form of fixed deposit with the attraction that interest paid was not subject to withholding tax. This form of borrowing was not only expensive, but also had to be retired immediately upon maturity. On the other hand accommodations and loans were effortlessly arranged with banks within a group, with somewhat looser settlement arrangements. Such loans appear neither to have been assessed nor negotiated on an arm's-length basis. One of the entities in the group needed cash, and that was that. What is perhaps more difficult to explain in hindsight is insurance companies' solution of issuing ever more lump-sum, interest-sensitive policies when they needed cash. A lump-sum, interest-sensitive policy includes about 1% insurance,[26] it takes effect by an initial lump-sum payment, and earns an interest rate that is unrelated to performance of any specified investment or set of investments. The lump-sum, interest-sensitive policies portfolio of Jamaica Mutual Life Assurance Society, for instance, was $2.1 billion of which only $168 million—merely 0.8% was insurance coverage. The number of lump-sum policy holders was 6,513. To choose expanded issuance of these policies as a solution would, on inspection, appear more like digging one hole to fill another, robbing Peter to pay Paul. But this behaviour fits perfectly within our scenario of "euphoria," "me-tooism" and unwarranted optimism discussed earlier. Mutual Life created "Mutual Investor Plus"; Crowne Eagle created "Asset Investor"; and Dyoll Life created "Fortune". The very names of these vehicles suggest the mindset of market optimism sold by the image makers and the prevailing "quick capital gain" attitude quoted from the Bank of Jamaica in our introduction.

There is yet another seldom-discussed element of causation associated with the general level of speculative euphoria evident in Jamaican investment behaviour in the late 1980s to early 1990s. Radio talk shows are ubiquitous in Jamaica. In total they would take up perhaps more than 90% of airtime in any one twenty-four-hour period if their hours of exposure were combined across the different radio stations. These shows in general, but one very popular morning show in particular, *The Breakfast Club*, became a kind of forum for discussions on the economy, business developments, the stock market, and investment in general. Often, the principals of the subsequently failed, but then prevailing high-flying institutions, newspaper commentators on financial matters, accountants, "economic analysts," and investment advisors would parade their skills, wisdom, and unique or esoteric expertise in the field. TV programmes on finance and investment were also developed, which more or less mirrored these subjects discussed on the radio talk shows. Investment seminars became commonplace. Partly because of the marketing of new stock issues and divestments undertaken by the government, a larger number of persons became interested in "playing the market."

In a remarkably uncanny parallel, Galbraith cites Professor Dice's 1929 observation of the United States speculative bubble:

> The common folks believe in their leaders. We no longer look upon the captains of industry as magnified crooks. Have we not heard their voices over the radio? Are we not familiar with their thoughts, ambitions, and ideals as they have expressed them to us almost as a man talks to his friend. [Galbraith then comments] Such a feeling of trust is essential for a boom. When people are cautious, questioning, misanthropic, suspicious, or mean, they are immune to speculative enthusiasm.[27]

The similarities abound! The major players in the Jamaican financial sector were being referred to as "captains of industry," and were often on radio and TV shows performing "almost as a man talks to his friend." There was a general "get-rich-quick" feeling in the air. It is these conditions that allowed depositors to place funds with a bank, small, new, and obviously with no track record, yet expecting several points higher in interest rates, never questioning the capacity of the institution to deliver.[28] The people were not "cautious, questioning, misanthropic, suspicious, or mean." As a result they had no immunity to speculative enthusiasm, and the Jamaican indigenous financial services sector encouraged and spearheaded the speculative bubble.

Regardless of controversy surrounding the causes of the crisis and government's decision to intervene, any independent or disinterested reading and diagnostic of the events leading to the collapse cannot but conclude that the crisis exhibited all the classic signs, admittedly with the element of uniqueness described earlier. The government's resolution agency, FINSAC, commissioned and undertook several independent diagnostic reviews, carried out by both local and overseas-based professionals. The international firms Ernest and Young, McKinsey, and Price Waterhouse were among providers of consultancy services. These studies undertaken by completely disinterested parties unearthed almost the complete range of problems associated with crises in general. Failures identified by these sources, with brief descriptions, explanations, and the author's additional comments, are intermingled where appropriate in the bulleted list that follows.[29]

The list of problems is comprehensive:

• *Absence of, or failure to comply with, proper internal control procedures*

The troubled banks showed a high incidence of fraud and irregularities, indicating weak control mechanisms. Loan documentation was often not perfected, and in some cases titles to property used as collateral could not be found. In effect, a practice had developed in the sector to have borrowers sign documentation which was then not registered with the relevant governmental agencies, nor were required stamp duties paid. The result was that lenders' interests were sometimes not protected in law. It is not clear whether this practice was developed to save borrowers money or was simply an internal control failure. In some instances, documentation simply could not be located, even though they were supposed to be in secure facilities of banks' vaults.

• *Poor risk management and inadequate portfolio diversification*

Absence of these elements of financial management resulted in a high ratio of bad loans and insufficient portfolio diversification, as evidenced by unacceptably high exposure to single borrowers and/or single industries. Further compounding the situation was the fact that, where portfolio diversification did actually occur, it took place in areas for which the banks had no competencies. Group structures allowed banks to fund risky ventures within the group—connected parties. In instances, these privately owned financial entities behaved as if they worked with the mandate of a government-subsidized development bank.

• *High and increasing levels of non-performing assets*

Due to inadequate investment assessment and monitoring, there were increasing levels of non-performing assets. In not matching the maturity of assets and liabilities, banks became excessively vulnerable to movement in asset prices, interest and exchange rates.

• *High operating costs*

The troubled banking institutions were inefficient, requiring large spreads between lending and deposit rates. Jamaican spreads rose from 1992–1994 levels of 14%–15% to 21%–22% in 1995–1997. This compared to spreads of 7%–8% in Barbados, Guyana, and Trinidad and Tobago during the same period, 1992–1997. Indigenous banks argued that larger spreads were needed to compensate for higher liquidity reserve requirements, averaging around 48% of deposit liabilities, compared to half this percentage in Guyana and Trinidad and Tobago and 39% in Barbados in the period between 1993 and 1997. Larger spreads pushed up interest rates and, in some instances, compounded customers' problems related to their indebtedness and inability to pay, thereby contributing to growth in bad debt. A World Bank study of 132 countries ranked Jamaica's interest rate spread of 19.1% in 1998 as the seventh highest in the world.

• *Poor quality of management and strategic planning*

The indigenous banks had negative return on assets (ROAs) compared with positive, although declining ROAs of 2%–3.5%, as was occurring in the foreign banks operating in Jamaica.

• *Failure to exercise due diligence and care*

Financial institutions operated in the absence of sound corporate governance practices and with limited involvement of their boards of directors. Rather than demonstrated expertise, experience, or capacity to bring true independence and unique value to board decisions, board membership sometimes merely reflected friendships, reward for past favours, and the "buddy" syndrome.

• *Unusually high appetite for risk*

Most local financial sector entrepreneurs have been cited as being too quick to risk depositors' funds, too eager to exhibit the trappings of success in their competition with each other, hence the "edifice complex," and too prone to bend prudential norms and regulations.

• *A high incidence of connected party lending*

As depositors withdrew funds placed in lump-sum, interest-sensitive policies, insurance companies tapped into their affiliated banks for funds to meet these withdrawal demands, inevitably weakening the banks. When the insurance company in the group was unable to repay these loans, the banks failed.

• *Breach of fiduciary duty and fraud*

Several files were turned over to the Director of Public Prosecution, indicating forensic evidence of fraud and breach of fiduciary duty, among other crimes.

This list could easily represent the "proscribed" in an introductory Power-Point presentation to students of finance. As the basic ingredients causing the crisis, the evidence unmistakably points to a failure in responsible financial management of the indigenous financial services sector—in all its diverse areas—coupled with a lax regulatory environment; exhibition of a herd instinct in going after unsustainably rising prices (asset values) among investors, borrowers, and speculators; greed; absence of fiduciary responsibility; unwise government divestments or privatization; and fraud. The order in which these factors are listed does not in any way imply the relative importance of the issue—they contributed in unison and simultaneously to produce the ultimate crash. To assign a ranking would be an exercise in pure speculation. It can be said with confidence, however, that macroeconomic and monetary policy aimed at stemming the boom in credit creation and inflation exposed the unsustainable condition of the institutions, precipitating and laying bare the situation, but not causing the crash.

The psychology of the speculator/investor, the herd instinct moving for quick gains, was of course the necessary euphoric glue holding together the visions that allow normally cautious or prudent people to get carried away with possibilities that ascend to certainty in a mere flash of the mind's eye. Only the indigenous institutions ended up distressed. This fact inevitably leads one to the depressing but overwhelming conclusion that the crisis could have been avoided. Mild but timely application of prudential control would have achieved this. The foreign banks' head offices made the big decisions and managed prudential standards—they survived the meltdown. The authorities' major failure was not anti-inflationary monetary and fiscal policy; it was their acceptance of the notion of liberalization and the creation of a liberalized environment that allowed so many small and capital-poor financial institutions to mushroom without simultaneously modernizing the legal, institutional, regulatory, and remedial capabilities of the overseeing institutions. This conclusion, however, became discernible to many only in the blinding clarity of hindsight.

It should however be pointed out that it does not appear to be the case that the indigenous entrepreneurs approached their activities with questionable intent. They all seemed to have been innovative and entrepreneurial—as we saw in the comparable episodes, particularly the Lehman investment bank described earlier—in creation of institutions to achieve their goals. The set of unfortunate events then precipitated desperate behaviors. These included fraudulent activities which were allowed to prevail by outmoded rules and their associated lax regulatory oversight system. The inevitable outcome was the resultant crash.

2

The Gathering Storm: Bankruptcy at Blaise and Century National Bank

TEMPORARY MANAGEMENT: BLAISE TRUST AND MERCHANT BANK LTD.

Blaise Trust and Merchant Bank Ltd. was the first of the indigenous institutions in the modernized financial services sector to go under. This had more to do with irregularities and questionable transactions than merely imprudent management. The Minister of Finance intervened, assuming "Temporary Management" of the institution on December 18, 1994. This was rapidly followed by the public emergence of problems in Century National Bank and Workers Bank—all three, indigenous financial institutions.

Patrick Hylton, who was to later assume the position of CEO at FINSAC in 1998, had been appointed managing director of Blaise Trust and Merchant Bank in November of 1994. Upon review of the bank's accounts, it became clear that the institution was insolvent. This condition, as mandated by law, was reported to Governor Bussierres of the Bank of Jamaica and to the Minister of Finance.[30] The fact is however, Bank of Jamaica and the Finance Ministry were already aware of the situation, though not to the finest detail. Yet, they were desperately trying to resolve it. They were not fully aware of the problems due to the fact that the trust and merchant bank was associated with the Blaise Building Society. Regulatory arbitrage was practiced here, as building societies were not among the institutions in the BOJ regulatory net—the enabling legislation was yet to come. From their vantage point of overseeing the merchant bank, their early view was that the company needed a capital injection. Recapitalization of the institution would enable it to continue as a going concern and avoid deterioration of confidence in the financial system.

Blaise made elaborate efforts to achieve the numbers and ratios that would conform to this recommendation. A scheme was arranged in which an independent foreign investor[31] would inject new funds into Blaise Trust and Merchant Bank. The investor company, as revealed in court documents, was Continental Petroleum, incorporated in the Bahamas. The scheme was structured simply. Another connected company, this one incorporated in the Cayman Islands, West Euro Equities, borrowed US$1.3 million from Continental Petroleum. This loan was secured by guarantee of another company, Consolidated Holdings Ltd., which was associated with Blaise Trust and Merchant Bank by virtue of common shareholding. There was also a form of security in a mortgage over the Blaise Industrial Park, a commercial real estate property, controlled by another of the companies associated with Blaise. The interest rate on this loan was 24% at a time when U.S. interest rates were in the high single or very low double digits. This was a golden deal. Blaise guaranteed the loan in Jamaica, on the basis that it would pay a dividend of 24% on the money to enable West Euro Equities to make its repayments; otherwise it would be in default. This transaction as it occurred between Continental Petroleum and West Euro Equities was never disclosed to the Bank of Jamaica. What was thought of as an investor putting capital at risk was really a collateralized loan.

These efforts at "recapitalization" failed. Financial Institution Services (FIS), the vehicle created to manage the assets and payout of Blaise depositors, challenged this transaction in the courts, arguing that it should not repay the US$1 million loan camouflaged as an investment. The FIS view was that an investment presumes risk, hence there could be no implied cover, no guaranteed return on capital. One of the problems of litigation, however, is the time and expense associated with reaching a binding decision. The overwhelming view of legal experts therefore suggested repayment should be made, thus giving rise to an earlier settlement. The elaborate scheme to create an "injection" of capital, the funds of a new, previously unconnected investing partner, was recognized and defined by the court, as in reality, a collateralized loan. This episode is recounted here to indicate the kind of behaviour which those with fiduciary responsibility exhibited. Instead of regulatory arbitrage, the improper but nevertheless legal device we discussed earlier, the bank was indeed making patently false claims to regulators.

Blaise had an interesting history, shared in some respects by at least one other of the failed institutions. One mechanism for establishing a financial stable was the purchase of an institution that was already legally on the books, licensed but perhaps dormant or non-functioning. Blaise Trust was created in 1956 as a trust company. It was later converted into a merchant bank and trust company in 1987 as "Blaise Trust and Merchant Bank." Its forerunner, however, had existed for a much longer period. It was formerly an entity associated with predecessors of the law firm Nunes Scholefield DeLeon in 1940s Jamaica. At that time, in the context of an underdeveloped financial structure and nonexistent capital market locally, lawyers were routinely engaged in the business of managing clients' funds. To streamline their financial activities, lawyers would create trust companies providing financial intermediary services to their more affluent clients. In the 1940s and well into the latter half of the twentieth century, these funds under management were considerable in Jamaica. A natural consequence of this was that lawyers and law firms carried out significant financial intermediation activities—they developed mortgage portfolios. What became Blaise Trust and Merchant Bank Ltd. was also at an earlier stage owned by a prominent Montego Bay businessman.

The company was purchased, and its operations expanded in scope. It operated both its merchant bank and building society from offices at 9 Trinidad Terrace in New Kingston. The main point of note here is that prior to the Banking Act of 1992 such an institution could change hands by private sale independent of Bank of Jamaica scrutiny or approval. Current Bank of Jamaica regulations require a person to pass the "fit and proper" test—to have no criminal record, to have not been a bankrupt, and so on—in order to operate a financial institution. Blaise at that time was therefore licensed to operate without having to undergo any of this scrutiny. It was not one of the earliest "groups" formed, but its structure reflected the prevailing wisdom of the day. Blaise Trust and Merchant Bank Ltd. had a subsidiary: Blaise Investments Ltd., which apparently (given the details available at the time of its problems in 1994) owned Lex Insurance Brokers Ltd. In the "group" there was also Blaise Building Society and a company called Consolidated Holdings Ltd., which in turn owned Melmond Ltd. The author made no effort to chronicle the operations of these entities. The point is merely to illustrate the pattern and simplicity of creation of an interlocking group. Prior to the Finance Minister's assumption of "Temporary Management" in 1994,

> Blaise Trust and Merchant Bank Ltd. showed signs of weakness in its overall performance. However, because of the legal limitations under the then existing statute, (The Protection of Depositors Act), **the supervisory authorities were prevented from imposing remedial measures upon an institution that was following imprudent practices**. Supervisory initiatives mainly took the form of moral suasion. Although this had varying levels of success, the core

problems of poor loan quality, (particularly loans to related parties which were non-performing) weak administration, ineffective internal controls and inadequate accounting records remained largely unaddressed. These concerns of the Bank of Jamaica, were also corroborated by the merchant bank's own external auditors, David A. Wong and Company.[32]

Clear evidence of the destruction of the firewall between financial institutions with different objectives, rules, regulatory regimes, and clientele is to be seen in this comment of the Minister to Parliament:

The operations of Blaise Building Society were affected by the assumption of Temporary Management of the Merchant Bank because **although it is a separate legal entity, it occupied the same premises and employed the same staff as the merchant bank.**[33]

In effect, the distinction between the two operations was merely on paper, purely for 'apparent' compliance with existing law.

In his report of October 1995 on the activities and financial condition of the Blaise Building Society, the inspector had this to say:

It would appear from the investigation that Donald Panton, Janet Panton, Orett Hutchinson, Edwin Douglas, Jeremiah Edwards and T. John Francis were important participants in bringing about the parlous position of the society....[I]t appears that the society was operated for the benefit of the Pantons and related entities/persons with little regard for the obligations created through the solicitation of funds from the public.

It is clear that attempts have been made to take advantage of weaknesses in the Jamaica Companies Act. The Pantons appear to have hidden their ownership of certain companies and other assets behind nominee shareholders in an effort to deflect responsibility. Note in particular the cases of Unijam and DJNJ.

Several of the Panton companies come [*sic*] across during the investigation have not filed timely returns with the Registrar or have filed no returns. Accordingly, it proved difficult to identify the persons having responsibility for the actions of each company.[34]

The comments on weaknesses in the Companies Act and late or absent filing of returns, as this quote indicates, is clear evidence of regulatory laxity. The system, for whatever reason, be it a matter of overburden or something other, allowed these breaches to go unchecked.

Blaise had much earlier engaged in practices to grow and expand its capital and reserve, based on unrealized surpluses derived from asset revaluation—internal book entries. This practice is absolutely imprudent for such a financial institution, particularly when the expanded or notional capital is the result of inflationary trends. In this situation capital was the base used to determine the level of deposits, which, as a licensed institution, it was legally entitled to accept. As early as 1986 and 1987, the Bank of Jamaica inspectors recommended either removing the appropriate values from the capital structure, or reducing the level of deposits. Around the same time, credit to connected parties or institutions either parent or subsidiary in the group structure appeared to be stretching the bounds of prudential administration. Collateral securities on these loans were untraceable, credit files and documentation were inadequate or nonexistent, and principal payments continued way behind schedule. Funds treated as liquid assets were often not in effect liquid, as they were hypothecated (pledged) as security for indebtedness. The unmistakable impression to be had from the company's accounting and financial practices was one of using whatever loophole necessary, prudent or imprudent, permissible but inappropriate, to continue operations until some unknown moment in the future when speculative asset values would be realized. In financial circles this is known as "the greater fool theory": with just a bit more waiting, there will always be someone else willing to pay a higher price for the asset. This greater fool theorem predominates and becomes contagious among speculators during any kind of euphoric boom.

Finally, in the face of the company's insolvency and impending closure, a new government entity, Financial Institutions Services Ltd. (FIS), was created to deal with the payout of depositors whose funds were held in the building society and merchant bank. Such assets as existed became available to FIS. Even a brief perusal of the operations of this "group" demonstrates that a highly speculative approach to investment prevailed. Connected parties were funded to engage in ventures that might have a future, but for which sufficient capital was neither in place nor could, reasonably, ever be envisaged as being readily forthcoming. These included the exotic Navy Island, former playground of film star Errol Flynn, several real estate holdings in different phases of completion, and sundry other speculations. The loans enabling purchase of these ventures were, for the most part, non-performing for years.

TEMPORARY MANAGEMENT: CENTURY NATIONAL BANK

Century National Bank had been allowed to run up large overdrafts at the Bank of Jamaica to the tune of $4 billion. Even with this level of assistance, it was unable to meet its obligations. It was also unable to recapitalise itself, and in consequence, the Minister of Finance attempted to broker a deal with other indigenous financial institutions thought to be in a position to come to its rescue by way of a merger. These institutions included the Horizon Financial and United General Insurance Groups. The talks and negotiations, in the small society that Jamaica is, were anything but secret. Both print and electronic media were onto them in a flash. Indeed, minutes after leaving a meeting at Jamaica House,[35] one of the principals of the distressed institution was on his cell phone to a radio talk show, discussing the nature of the problems associated with the contemplated merger—including, of course, a great deal of the substance of the meeting.

Perhaps inevitably, negotiations broke down. The principals of the indigenous institutions involved in merger talks generally referred to themselves as the "Owners Club." Their attitude was that, whereas Jamaican managers of foreign-owned banking operations were merely employees, they were, on the contrary, autonomous players in the financial sector who were no longer dependent on decisions from abroad. At least one of them had his banking training at one of the foreign-owned banks. The personality and ego of Century's principal would always have been an impediment to any merger in which his stake would be diluted or made, in any way, inferior to another. Century generally created grand visions; its reach and importance was an offshoot of the principal, who tended to bask in the adoration of a public which knew of—or if it did not, had to be made aware of—his importance. This was not someone who would willingly give up control of his creation—even if the alternative could possibly be its ultimate demise.

On July 10, 1996, the Minister of Finance, invoking powers vested in him by the Banking Act, assumed "Temporary Management" of the Century National Bank. Simultaneously, Richard Downer, of the accounting firm Price Waterhouse, was appointed to manage the institutions in the Minister's behalf. Examination of the institution's books confirmed that there was an excess of liabilities over assets of the order of $2.5 billion. Further analysis of the affairs of the group indicated that balance sheet adjustments should be made to reflect the true state of the banks assets, particularly the loans. When collectibility of the loan portfolio was assessed, the true deficiency approached the order of $4.8 billion.[36] Effectively the bank was continuing to carry on its books loans that had been non-performing for excessively long periods of time.

It was clearly established that the institution was insolvent. Even the $4.8 billion figure could not be accurately ascertained since there was considerable uncertainty surrounding ownership of the most significant asset of the group—the Jamaica Grande—Jamaica's largest convention hotel. The Finance Minister's affidavit in Suit No. M 71 indicates the parlous state of affairs that had evidently existed for some time prior to the revelation of a condition of collapse. Examination of the group's books indicated, among other problems, the following issues:

- The board of directors and owners "have failed to conduct the business of the Respondent (CNB) according to law in all respects and prudently on behalf of the Depositors"

- Deposit liabilities exceeded limits prescribed by law

- Unsecured credit to directors exceeded limits prescribed by law

- Credit to persons exceeded limits prescribed by law

- Board of directors presented misleading financial statements

- Depositors' interest subordinated to owners via non-arms length transactions

But perhaps most damaging to any vision of a public financial institution enjoying the trust of depositors was the following:

> The state of the accounting and loan record is shocking and evidenced a laxity that seems negligent in nature. There are unreconciled suspense accounts of hundreds of millions of dollars and even bank accounts have not been regularly reconciled…events have evidenced that they have been incompetent, reckless, deceptive and cavalier and not deserving of the trust that was placed in them by depositors.[37]

I quote this particular conclusion of the Minister's affidavit in its entirety because it highlights some of the difficulties that would have had to be faced in any attempt at reconstruction. Reconstruction of an insolvent bank can proceed by taking out the worthless assets—bad loans—and restructuring the institution along the lines of the "good bank/bad bank" scenario.[38] When this is done, the objective is to restore and return the institution to financial and operational viability. Such would be the case if the basic cause of collapse were changing market conditions, genuine risk assessment errors, and panic among investors. With the state of affairs in evidence, however, even that scenario was rendered inappropriate.

As was the case with Blaise, so too for Century—the decision was mandated by the circumstances and condition of the institution. Depositors would be protected and payouts made. Financial Institution Services Ltd. (FIS), the company that had been established by government going forward from Blaise, would now also handle the payout of Century.

Investigation and review of the state of affairs at Century National Bank led to court proceedings. On August 2, 2001, fully five years after the institution was determined to be bankrupt and closed, the *Jamaica Daily Gleaner* reported under its front page headline, "Court Finds Fraud by Crawford," the following:

> It was the court's finding that Crawford committed "fraud" in the transaction concerning the house at Paddington Terrace, St. Andrew which he had purchased from Century National Bank in 1990....The Court of Appeal found that Crawford had knowledge that the market value of the property was $4million but he did not disclose that to the board of directors when he purchased the property. The property was sold for $1.8 million and transferred to Regardless Ltd., a company owned by Crawford, his wife and his children.[39]

Fraud and fiduciary irresponsibility often do emerge in instances as part of the scenario of collapse. It often involves the people at the top of the institution, whether it is top management or owner/managers. In this case it centred on non-disclosure of material facts to the company's board of directors, which would result in loss to the company and its shareholders. Most recently "Bernard J. Ebbers, founder and former chief executive of WorldCom...found guilty of fraud by a New York jury in March, agreed...to surrender nearly all his personal fortune—about [US]$40 million—to investors..." This in what has been described in the *New York Times* as the "biggest corporate fraud in history."[40] Ebbers had been lent "hundreds of millions of dollars to pay off loans backed by the shares"[41] after WorldCom stock had collapsed. Century National Bank's case exhibited similar symptoms—known information concealed from at least some of the board, to the detriment of shareholders and benefit of a principal.

But another, perhaps more interesting, element of the behaviour of some principals in Jamaica's indigenous financial services sector can be gleaned from the choice of names for vehicles used to accomplish some of their objectives. The name of Crawford's company involved in this transaction was "Regardless." One gets the impression that they knew the wrong they were committing, but this was a game in which winning was the only objective—at any cost. For some, the rule-book was flexible and the umpire handicapped. Another operative, in this case peripheral yet connected to the meltdown, proudly refers to himself in a letter to a client as being descended from Captain Morgan. He could not vouch for another who may have been descended from the Duke of Wellington. Morgan, the pirate of infamous connection to Jamaica's seventeenth-century "sin city," Port Royal, and Wellington, would of course share entirely conflicting views on the nature of the transaction they contemplated!

The impression that is difficult to avoid is that some principals seemed, for a significant period of their operations, effectively driven by amorality or immorality. This placed them above and beyond all rules in what was really a self-determined game—including an element of adolescent or sophomoric fun at the expense of those whom they knew they were outfoxing.

It is interesting to compare these behaviours with that of some of Enron's traders in the state of California. The Enron Corporation was both politically powerful in the United States and the darling of Wall Street until 2001. In the autumn of that eventful year, it imploded—its name, formerly associated with ever-rising stock values and surpassing the "Street's" expectations of quarterly profits, became synonymous with corporate scandal and wrongdoing. Enron was, among other things, a marketer of power whereas a connected party, Portland General, was a power generator. By law they were barred from dealing directly with each other in the state of California. If they colluded, they could drive up electricity prices. As Kurt Eichenwald describes it in his *Conspiracy of Fools*—a fascinating portrayal of the implosion and collapse of Enron—a trader by the name of Forney contacted the power scheduling desk at Portland General. He had developed an idea for using Portland General to

> transform lower-priced power from California into higher-priced out-of-state electricity. All that was required was a loop—buying electricity in California, passing it around through out-of-state trading companies and then to Portland General, which would deliver it back. The transactions were all on paper, but so much the better; traders could mark up the price at each stage, making a tidy profit courtesy of California consumers....The Forney Perpetual Loop, as the in-and-out trades came to be known, was only one of the schemes cooked up by Enron's traders...They all had cute names. One, Death Star, involved submitting fake transmission schedules that showed lines would be overloaded; Enron would then be paid for 'reducing' congestion by removing scheduled power it never meant to send. Another, Fat Boy, was a variation on the theme but allowed prices to drive up in anticipation of the coming fake

congestion. With Get Shorty, Enron pledged to line up backup reserves while in fact doing nothing, under the assumption that the reserves would never be needed. And Ricochet was another variation of the Forney Loop.[42]

These trades continued for some time before they were unearthed. When that occurred, upon discovery of the names Death Star, Fat Boy, and Ricochet, Enron's lawyers were in dismay. It almost didn't matter whether the methods Enron employed were legitimate or not, not with those kinds of names. Such in-your-face flamboyance would be enough to sway a jury. Topping it off, they were juvenile…sophomoric."[43] It appears that contemptuous gloating over those who were being knowingly and illegally fleeced, all in their blissful ignorance and trust, is good fun among those who played these games!

Returning to the court's judgment in this particular case, there were also comments on other elements of the problems at Century National Bank. The court found fraud to be

> disclosed on the face of the record; and no evidence having been offered to contradict it, the court must take cognizance of it particularly in these circumstances where fraud was committed by a person in a fiduciary position vis-à-vis the company that was defrauded. Such a person ought not to be allowed to shelter behind an Act of Parliament, to defeat the proprietary right of another who is the beneficial owner of the property.…The court found that the bank suffered great loss as a result of Crawford's negligence and breach of fiduciary duty. The court said that Crawford indulged in unwise banking practice, and apparently deliberately put the bank's funds at risk in order to assist companies in all of which he had direct personal interest.[44]

Another interesting finding of the court had to do with banking practice as evidenced by the actions of its managing director.

> It was the court's finding that…[the managing director]…was also responsible for the bank's losses.…[he]…ought to have known of the misapplication of the funds of the bank, but instead allowed payments to be made out of an **unwarranted loyalty** to Crawford.[45]

While the court perhaps has a duty to speak of an "unwarranted loyalty," its view could hold only in the abstract. These institutions always reflected the personality of their founder/owner. Loyalty to the boss was non-negotiable. The word of the boss was law. The managing director described by the court as having an "unwarranted loyalty" had been a manager at one of the international banks for many years. At that bank he would have had to be completely aware of and abide by their manuals of procedure. He knew what were, and were not, allowable expenditures. But in these institutions' systems, manuals of procedure were abandoned, checks and balances avoided, and pecking-order positions reigned.

3

Crisis Full Blown, Publicly Acknowledged

The activities of mid-1996 included the Minister of Finance assuming "Temporary Management" of Century National Bank, but more importantly, the Insurance sector began to acknowledge, both to itself and to the government, if not to the public at large, that it was in need of financial assistance. As they saw it, theirs was a liquidity problem. Their investments in underperforming real estate and a weak stock market, coupled with inappropriate products—for the state of affairs of the economy—encouraged early encashment. Inevitably the outcome was pressure on their liquidity. Encashment required compulsory sale of equities at precisely the time when heavy losses would be incurred. While staving off the inevitable, their short-term borrowings at high interest rates not only made more certain the outcome; they also made that outcome appear and converge closer on the horizon.

From the perspective of an observer, researcher, or the general public, an interesting question is: When was the crisis diagnosed? If you had to find a date for the crash, what would that date be? When did we know? Minister Davies, whose task it was to oversee this period of difficulty, was asked the following question: "When did it become clear that the indigenous financial services sector was indeed in crisis?" His response:

> Very hard to answer that definitively. At various points it was apparent that some institutions had serious difficulties but that is not abnormal, for example…former Governor Bussieres following the Blaise debacle and the Ministry of Finance assuming responsibility for regulating the Building Societies, up until that stage **the establishment of a Building Society was easier than getting a driver's license!** You simply got a form and filled it out; and there was nothing to prevent, in a sense the Registrar General who was called the Deputy Keeper of Records was obliged, you just paid for the form and you had a Building Society….Ministry of Finance established a law adjusting the Finan-

cial Institutions Act to prescribe Building Societies as one of the Institutions which had to be duly licensed. The issue of the existing Institutions came up and Bussieres, to give him full credit, indicated that he had doubts about Eagle and Century which had come from nowhere to be Nos. 3 and 4—just out of nowhere in a couple of years because simply what they were doing was diverting, attracting deposits into the Building Society because there were no reserve requirements etc. and he objected.[46]

The Minister does not give a date. But he certainly has a particular timeline in mind. Governor Bussieres was uneasy with the situation. Obviously the Minister did not divulge all that the governor would have discussed with him. But the existence of concern is clear from his answer. This gives us a clue—it was after the passage of the Financial Institutions Act of 1992. This places a limiting beginning date at December 1992, for this was the actual date of passage of the legislation. We could argue that the 1994 closure of Blaise Trust and Merchant Bank signaled the crisis. Yet others may suggest the closure of Century National Bank on July 10, 1996, would be the best date to assign to the actual crash. But a financial sector crash and a stock market crash, while they may share a similar set of behavioural and other determinants do have one significant difference—for the stock market there will be a day, perhaps even an hour, when everyone knows the market has plunged and crashed. For financial institutions or a financial services sector, conditions of collapse usually exist for some time before it becomes common knowledge such that a crash might be said to have occurred. Usually it is the professionals in treasury management, accountants, and auditors who are first to perceive symptoms of an incipient crash. If their communications to management do not result in corrective action, the slide continues. Considering this issue for Jamaica, one would have to place the time of crash at around the early months of 1996, certainly at the time of closure of Century National Bank in mid-1996.

While the Minister's response does not provide the crash diagnosis date, it does indicate the inadequacy of the regulatory mechanism associated with the existing legislation. It was demonstrably deficient in accomplishing the task. It also remained subject to regulatory arbitrage by institutions that were aligned, as these were, in the prevailing "group" structure. The practice of ever-greening loans and associated shifting of loans and deposits across institutions was opaque to the regulatory system under the old regime. The effect of this was that, if a routine Bank of Jamaica inspection found problems in the commercial or merchant bank of a group on one day, those same problems could be wiped off the next by what were *de facto* internal book entries. It was simply achieved by transference of the offending accounts and relationships to sister institutions not subject to inspection—regulatory arbitrage. As it then turned out, Bank of Jamaica recommended that building societies should all be licensed in order to bring them under the purview of the new regulatory system.

With this recommendation, however, a huge problem loomed. How could the Bank of Jamaica, even if a particular building society in one of the "stables" appeared to be in difficulties, refuse to grant a license to an institution that previously enjoyed the confidence of Jamaica's saving public? Such refusal might itself be cause for panic and crisis. This type of problem highlights the unique difficulties of regulating any financial system. The word "credit" derives from the Latin "*credere*"—to believe. Truth be told, the system rests upon a foundation of belief. Once the general population of account holders and clients of financial institutions believe their funds are safe, the system functions smoothly. Indeed, one writer likened financial systems to that of the plumbing in a skyscraper—operating properly, no one notices it; let it malfunction however and life becomes unbearable. The decision was therefore taken to license all the existing building societies, but to work with them to straighten out their difficulties.

The problem, however, was much wider and deeper than merely those of the building societies. Attempts to merge the indigenous financial entities mentioned earlier, contrary to popular opinion expressed in the Jamaican media, was not the idea of the Finance Minister. Rather the merger solution derived from the group of indigenous financial sector participants referred to earlier—the "Owners Club"—this group included Horizon, Caldon, Workers, and Century. Their and the Minister's initiative failed, leading to "Temporary Management" of Century National Bank, yet there were much greater difficulties to come.

Prior to assumption of "Temporary Management" at Century National Bank, the major insurance companies approached government with alarming news. Based on their internally generated projections, they faced a deep liquidity crisis requiring immediate support. They suggested that theirs was a liquidity problem caused by a mismatch of assets and liabilities. Their assessment was that the industry might need in the region of $3 billion. The financial crisis, for the government at least, now clearly had to be reckoned with. Until the magnitude of the crisis was known, the general public could not be involved. A response was now desperately needed. The response would require assessment of the scope of the problem, identification of funds and/or facilities to stem the liquidity crunch, and creation of credible arrangements that would not cause a loss of confidence in the financial services sector as a whole. With consulting assistance from international accounting and auditing firms, government established a task force to look at the problem, while requesting the companies to prepare their own operational turn-around plans.

It was quickly determined that their real problem was not merely insufficiency of liquidity but was rather a problem of solvency. These companies were linked within group structures to banks, merchant banks, and other types of financial institutions—the problem would be much wider than first appeared. The Minister of Finance approached the World Bank in early 1996 to discuss possibilities of assistance to deal with the problem—a problem the extent of which could not then be fully appreciated. As is perhaps too much of a normal practice among the multilaterals, the World Bank (International Bank for Reconstruction and Development—IBRD), as if in reflex action, thought the International Monetary Fund (IMF) should also be involved, and for good measure, so too should the Inter-American Development Bank (IADB).

In the nature of things, meetings to deal with this issue were arranged for Washington. In a society as small as Jamaica's, the presence of representatives of the major multilaterals for undisclosed meetings with the Ministry of Finance and Bank of Jamaica would automatically arouse suspicions of too many possibilities. Was the exchange rate to be devalued, was Jamaica going back to the IMF for balance of payments reasons, etc.? Private meetings avoided all of this. Yet they proved, if not barren, certainly too late and sparse in flowering. This was a clear failure of the multilaterals to come to the aid of a member state in distress. Several reasons account for their failure to respond quickly and positively.

First, the mandate of none of these institutions includes a requirement to assist with emergency conditions in a country's domestic financial services. The IMF has its focus on balance of trade, payments, exchange rates, and international issues; the World Bank and IADB, with developmental projects and issues. None of the institutions could therefore immediately commit to assistance in an intervention to prevent domestic financial sector collapse. Although there was the recent history of the Mexican intervention, the circumstances were entirely different.

Exposure of significant U.S. banks to Mexico and the potential effect that it could have on international investment elicited an immediate response from the United States itself—the notion being "too big to fail." The multilaterals would come in on the heels of whatever decisions their major contributor would have taken and implemented. To be as small as Jamaica, and therefore not a threat to the entire international financial system, meant the response of the multilaterals would be a cautious one—they would make every effort to be practical, risking no mistakes; in other words prolonged analysis and endless "talks" would ensue—an absolute necessity.

In the event, exactly this occurred. So much so that at one of the meetings scheduled to discuss what was supposed to be a confidential matter, the large number of multilaterals' representatives present made the whole notion of confidentiality an undisguised joke. One official with whom I spoke suggested that as many as forty participants from the multilaterals were present. Minister Davies had to face a stark reality—first, confidentiality was at stake; second, assistance would not be forthcoming in quantities remotely close to the sums required; and third, should assistance be offered, it would not come fast enough to meet the emergency. Jamaica would now really have to bite the bullet. The problem was systemic, but in a very special way. It was special in the sense that only the indigenous element of the financial services sector, admittedly a large part, was in crisis. The Bank of Nova Scotia, Citibank, Canadian Imperial Bank of Commerce—these were all doing business as usual.

FINSAC: GENESIS AND MISSION

Upon the insurance companies' approach to the Ministry of Finance to deal with their "liquidity problem occasioned by a mismatch of assets and liabilities" in April/May of 1996 and the formation of a task force to look into the problem, it was determined, as Bonnick recounts, that the issue was "insolvency—potential, borderline and in some cases substantial."[47] With hindsight always twenty-twenty, Bonnick's was an understatement. All the insurance companies were linked within a "group," or as in the case of Island Life Insurance Company and Victoria Mutual Building Society, tied to each other in a financial venture partnership. Jamaica Mutual Life Assurance Society was actually part owner of National Commercial Bank. Life of Jamaica owned Citizens Bank. Crown Eagle Life Insurance Company was associated with Eagle Commercial Bank and Eagle Merchant Bank, owned or participated in ownership of hotels and considerable real estate holdings, and owned and managed two unit trusts (mutual funds). Workers Bank had its beginnings during the period of democratic socialism in the mid-1970s as an independent entity geared toward meeting the needs of working people. Shortly after it was privatized, a group structure was created, making the bank part of a holding company—Corporate Group. The group's activities then expanded to include the hospitality business, real estate, insurance, and retail trade. Each of the entities in these groups maintained borrowing relationships within the group. Although not evident at the time of the crisis, the Horizon Group, spawned from its beginnings as Horizon Merchant Bank, was similarly structured and also deeply troubled.

Throughout the year 1996, the financial sector's condition and performance was in and out of the news headlines, on and off popular radio talk and TV shows. "Financial Analysts" (I use quotes here because it appeared that this qualification was created, conferred, or assumed by personal assertion or declaration of the one so described) appeared on talk shows indicating their "inside knowledge" of the perilous state of the insurance and banking institutions. It improves the status of the commentator to be privy to secret information. This leads to more requests to appear on shows. Some of them, apart from offering financial advice and investment services for gain, worked in the financial services sector itself.

While the former state of affairs presented remarkably clear conflict of interest, it remained quite a cheap—indeed without charge—and very effective form of advertising and public relations for those purporting to be financial analysts and advisors. Rumours of collapse proliferated immediately prior to "Temporary Management" of Century National Bank. Jamaica's political rivalry adverted to before did not help. The opposition (Jamaica Labour Party—JLP—at the time) leader had to field allegations that he had ceased servicing a debt to Century National Bank, while the Peoples National Party—PNP—would have to respond to charges that it had negotiated an electoral campaign loan with Century National Bank when, simultaneously, the government's Ministry of Finance was in official though confidential discussions with the bank—one that could candidly only be described as "in distress." In these circumstances it was no surprise that there was a run on one of the banks—Citizens Bank—in October of 1996; another occurred in 1997. In face of the reality of a deteriorating situation and the fact that the multilaterals would not provide immediate financial support for resolution of the problem, government acted. Toward the end of 1996, it became evident that the crisis could no longer be managed by *ad hoc* measures.

A decision was taken to create an institution, to some extent similar to the Resolution Trust Corporation that had been used by the U.S. Government in 1989 to resolve its Savings and Loan Crisis. The U.S. institutions in distress, commonly referred to as S&Ls, had been around from the time of Franklin Roosevelt's New Deal. They were meant to encourage home ownership as federally chartered savings and loan associations, taking deposits and granting residential mortgage loans. When they had to sell off mortgages to meet liquidity requirements in a changed interest rate environment, they became insolvent.[48] As we have suggested earlier, financial crises generally share many features in common. There are many similarities between what Jamaica faced and the S&L problem. There was thus no need to reinvent a Jamaican wheel, even if its radius would be different.

The notably interesting feature of government's decision rests squarely on the centrality of money and the uniqueness of banks and financial services in a modern economy. If a supermarket fails, that may well be, and usually is, good news for its competitor across the street. In financial services however, nothing could be further from the truth. Failure of one could, and normally would, depending upon its size or market share, lead to contagion and systemic collapse. Jamaica's Financial Secretary, Shirley Tyndall, in discussing the basis of government's decision, put one element of the problem most graphically:

> [G]overnment was more interested in the depositors...when we looked at the profile of people who got burnt in Blaise, there were people who had worked, who had saved, they were like retired civil servants, retired teachers, doctors, nurses, poor people and they found themselves penniless, more or less. They couldn't go to the supermarket, etc.,...we realized there were really some small people who were just saving, saving, and saving...their life savings that would have been lost. Similarly with the insurance sector, so then we realized that we had to step in to provide some sort of assistance.[49]

Thus the decision was taken at two levels: first, to rescue the financial sector in support of the economy as a whole; and second, the Jamaican social fabric could not survive devastation of the means of livelihood of such a wide cross section of the population. The institutions facing collapse were a significant part of the financial structure of the economy, with a large proportion of total deposit funds, pension holdings under management, and insurance contracts. The distressed insurance companies held policies for approximately half a million persons, with a combined sum assured in the region of $341 billion. These facts carried implications that government could not ignore. Late in 1996, with the decision to create a resolution institution already taken, someone had to be found to lead it.

It was quickly determined that Dr. Gladstone Bonnick, a Jamaican who had worked at the World Bank for many years, had once headed Jamaica's National Planning Agency (currently the Planning Institute of Jamaica), and had served for a short period as governor of the Bank of Jamaica, would be asked to head the institution. Bonnick had previously served as one of the Coke Commissioners, presenting a dissenting minority report.[50] Perhaps more importantly, Bonnick held the distinction of publicly maintaining the view, in the highly charged political atmosphere of democratic socialism of the late 1970s, that depreciation and devaluation meant one and the same thing in face of controversy over former Prime Minister Michael Manley's making a distinction between the two for what appeared at the time to be political purposes. He was indeed a Jamaican who would be seen as abundantly competent, qualified, independent, and fair-minded—put in its most general terms an "honest broker"—and indeed, additionally, a fearless one. Such a man could head and lend credibility to the institution that would grow so large, so fast, and touch so many lives on the most sensitive of issues.

With respect to a name for the entity, Bonnick, as first chairman of FINSAC's board and chief executive officer indicates:

> For reasons which I never understood, the initials IRS were being recommended. As an American resident and taxpayer, this name did not appeal to me. My view was that the name for this new body should clearly tell the world exactly what we were about. My suggestion was the Financial Sector Adjustment Company, which would conveniently shorten to FINSAC.[51]

For the purposes of this narrative, further and repeated attempts on my own part to determine derivation of the initials "IRS" as the name for the institution turned up nothing. Documents, including correspondence between troubled institutions and personnel who would later take on specific roles at FINSAC, do make reference to the institution as IRS. The initials IRS also occur in correspondence between some of the major consulting firms and advance teams that were later to be included among FINSAC's staff and paid consultants. Bonnick's initial and continuing discomfort with the initials IRS of course stems from its meaning in the United States—Internal Revenue Service, the taxman.

The Financial Sector Adjustment Company, FINSAC Ltd. was created on January 29, 1997, with mission "to build for Jamaica a financial sector that is stable, sound, strong, well regulated."[52]

GOVERNMENT'S PLEDGE AND MORAL HAZARD

With the difficult decisions taken and a strategy projected, the Prime Minister announced to Parliament on February 7, 1997, that the Jamaican government would guarantee depositors' funds in licensed deposit-taking institutions, pension funds managed by authorized institutions, and policyholders' funds in insurance companies. At that time no one knew for certain the extent of the financial support that would be required—it would not be exaggerating to say that the distressed institutions themselves were for the most part clueless on the matter! This immediately produces a dilemma. To restore confidence in the financial sector, a policy statement such as this is absolutely necessary, indeed, mandatory. But the blanket government guarantee tied the hands of the resolution institution—whereas deposits (liabilities) would hold all value, loans (assets) would have to be reworked or sold for what the market would bear. Once government assumed such an undertaking, the burden to perform was, in a very real sense, lifted from distressed institutions. At the same time, principals do not relinquish control over the enterprise. This is a classic case of what is referred to in finance as moral hazard—the situation in which asymmetric information prevails between two parties to a transaction, with implications for their behaviour and ultimate liability.

Here is a government guarantee, made in advance of having complete knowledge of the true state of the financial condition of the institutions whose insolvency makes the guarantee necessary in the first place. If the principals of these institutions choose not to act in good faith, there is no immediate way around this problem. In addition, the principals themselves may not be fully aware of their institutions' true financial condition. Remarkably, several of the troubled institutions either severely underestimated or under-represented their need for support.

FINSAC: PROTOCOLS AND MODE OF OPERATION

Board membership of FINSAC included individuals with combined experience of a number of years in public affairs, finance, economics, insurance, tourism and the hospitality industry, accounting and auditing, diplomatic practice, trade union and human resource management, negotiation practice, and the law. Roughly a third of the membership was female. Members who served included: Gladstone Bonnick, first chairman and CEO; the late Hon. Kenneth Rattray, OJ, QC; second chairman, Audrey Anderson; Dennis Boothe; Hon. David Coore, OJ, QC; Patrick Hylton, Managing Director; Derrick Lattibeaudierre; Hope Markes; Kemorine Miller; Lascelles Perry; Wilberne Persaud (the author); Senator Frank Pringle; Hon. Shirley Tyndall, OJ, CD; and David Wan. Secretaries to the FINSAC board included Wayne Whittingham, Lisa Shields, Celia Blake, and Julie Thompson—all practiced attorneys.

From the beginning the gravity of the crisis was fully grasped by the board. Any institution such as FINSAC, in any country in the world, would be second-guessed, having both its supporters and detractors. This was also fully grasped by the membership. There were multiple objectives. First was to create an efficient organization, operating on the strongest moral, ethical, and business principles. Second was to provide as much transparency as allowable in sensitive financial matters. Third was to treat every case on the basis of equity and fairness, making sure that like cases received like treatment. Fourth was to seek out and acquire the best advice from the finest professionals available to the country. Finally an accurate record had to be created for posterity. The fact that FINSAC's decisions would affect the lives of a large cross section of Jamaican society further reinforced the mandate that there be transparency in its operations.

Jamaica was embarking upon a road it had, fortunately, never before had to travel. There was thus no local road map, no previous experience to rely on. So the board had to determine to operate on the basis of general principles as those just mentioned as well as the experience of other countries' crisis-resolution schemes. If, for instance, an asset had to be valued for sale, the valuation would have to be done by at least two licensed professionals. Any actions of the company would have to conform to the principles agreed by the board.

FINSAC: TERMS OF REFERENCE AND OBJECTIVES

Terms of Reference:

1. FINSAC serves as the vehicle through which realignment and restructuring of the financial sector will take place.

2. FINSAC serves as the executive arm of the Ministry of Finance and Planning in which Government strategy will be planned and through which the interventions of various agencies (specifically the Bank of Jamaica (BOJ) and the Superintendent of Insurance) will be coordinated.

3. Through FINSAC, the Government will provide financial assistance to the sector and therefore FINSAC will have the accountability for spending of such resources provided to it directly or guaranteed by the Government.

4. Through FINSAC the Government will provide guidance and technical assistance to the financial sector. It may mobilize and deploy external technical and managerial support for the restructuring of intervened institutions.

5. FINSAC will sponsor and/or undertake diagnostic studies of the overall health of the financial sector with specific focus on the institutions which require assistance.

6. FINSAC will assist institutions in developing workout plans, where necessary, to return them to viability. Such plans will form the basis for conditions which FINSAC will attach to financial assistance. FINSAC will monitor the implementation of such plans on a continuing basis and will evaluate their effectiveness in achieving their specified objectives. It will inform and coordinate the inputs of FINSAC's board members of intervened institutions on issues considered essential to the viability of individual institutions within the sector.

7. Based on experience gained in its work, FINSAC will advise the Government on the prudential regulation of the sector and on the renewal, suspension, and revocation of operating charters of individual institutions within the sector.[53]

Objectives:

- To protect the investments of policyholders, depositors, and pensioners

- To restore liquidity and solvency to distressed institutions (in pursuit of the first objective)

- To strengthen the financial management capability of intervened institutions

- To improve the efficiency of the sector in mobilizing and allocating financial resources

- To create an attractive environment for investors to recapitalise financial institutions

- To minimize moral hazard and promote prudent behaviour

- To promote strong corporate governance, managerial accountability, and shareholder oversight

- To strengthen the sector through the establishment of appropriate institutional frameworks and regulatory structures

Due to the fact that the multilaterals would initially provide no financial support for rehabilitation but rather, only limited funding for technical assistance, FINSAC, at inception, envisaged four sources of finance for its operations:

- Domestic borrowing through sale of long-term local registered stock

- Issue of FINSAC notes[54] guaranteed by the government

- Sale proceeds from liquidation of assets and recoveries against non-performing loans purchased, including final sale of rehabilitated institutions

- Government funding of any shortfall at the end of its operations

The latter of course deriving from the fact that it was government that backed or guaranteed the FINSAC notes.

FINSAC: STRATEGIC PLAN

In order to give effect to its mandate and mission, FINSAC had to consider three stages for its activities: intervention, rehabilitation, and divestment. From the very beginning, the notion was to create an institution that would neither own in perpetuity nor control assets normally to be found in the private sector. Its proposed life cycle would be seven years. Intervention would take the form of an injection of capital necessary to protect the categories outlined in the government policy—depositors, pensioners, and the insured. In return for its capital injection, FINSAC would acquire from the distressed institution some combination of the following: representation on the board of directors, equity participation to a minimum of 26.5%,[55] and other assets, including non-performing loans. On occasion, intervention meant closure of an institution. In such cases, FINSAC would assume the deposit liabilities of the institution, simultaneously placing matching funds at a solvent, functioning institution for payout of the depositors.

These arrangements were necessary because FINSAC became *de facto* lender of last resort for distressed institutions, with the added responsibility of being receiver where necessary and restorer of viability where possible. We have become familiar, in the case of IMF lending, with the idea of "conditionalities." If agreed conditionalities are unmet, disbursement of funds is halted, frozen. In similar manner, FINSAC had to have forms of conditionality. In committing taxpayer support, a major objective was to ensure that viability was not merely feasible, but to the extent possible in a world of uncertainty, guaranteed. Board membership in an intervened entity provided some form of control, however mild. But such control could work only if owners and managers of distressed institutions maintained good faith. It would be contractual agreements with conditions precedent that provided a more bankable guarantee of working. The modality from the outset was to intervene by negotiation. Taking the approach by the insurance companies, reports of the task force, and further analysis by FINSAC consultants and the institutions themselves as a starting point, agreement was reached on specific programmes of assistance. These could contain one or more elements of the strategy leading either to closure or rehabilitation.

FINSAC: Asset Acquisition, Management, and Divestment

FINSAC would acquire assets, both financial and physical, as a result of its intervention in the sector. It would have to do all in its power to maintain their values, achieve appropriate professional valuations, and dispose of them at the best possible market price. To this end an asset management and divestment division was established in September 1998. The division was given a specific charter:

- Speedily dispose of assets acquired through the government of Jamaica's intervention in the financial sector

- Rehabilitate non-performing loans acquired by FINSAC

- Oversee the divestment process by intervened institutions that undertake their own disposal of assets

- Efficiently manage and maintain, until sale, all such assets

The financial institutions in which FINSAC intervened, in most cases by virtue of their possession of collateral that secured loans in default, owned substantial amounts of real estate and other assets. Indeed the fact that some of these assets were underperforming was reason for the troubled state of the institutions and, quite often, that of their clients too—resulting in FINSAC intervention in the first place. FINSAC would have to take the responsibility for divestment of these assets. In the case of non-performing loans purchased, mechanisms would have to be created either for their rehabilitation or for recovery of what could be salvaged in each specific situation.

Initially, FINSAC purchased non-performing loans from the banks but left them "physically" in the distressed bank. If, for instance, loans were bought from NCB, the documentation and files would still be maintained at NCB's offices. That bank would undertake to make collections even though the loans were no longer on its books as assets. Interestingly, one of the banks wanted a percentage of all collections to be paid to their officers who would be assigned to work on such collections—this, of course, was not approved by FINSAC.

FINSAC: STANDARD POLICY FOR NON-PERFORMING LOANS

As soon as the requisite staff, office space, and arrangements were in place, FINSAC took physical possession of the non-performing loans it had purchased and continued the "workout" process in-house. The guiding principles were established in the FINSAC "Standard Policy For Non-Performing Loans Workout." One of these guiding principles was preference for rehabilitation of loans rather than collateral asset sales. It was however recognized that the latter would prove inevitable in some cases to offset FINSAC's cost of loan purchases. The "key principles" set out by FINSAC to guide the operations of the loan recovery unit are set out below:[56]

- FINSAC is not a bank and is therefore unable to extend further credit—except in cases where loans already purchased have a commitment from the originating institution. In such instances, FINSAC will not continue said disbursement unless adequate security is in place and the debtor acknowledged the additional facility by way of Letter of Commitment, et al.

- FINSAC must ensure consistent treatment of all debtors in the portfolio.

- FINSAC's charter is for a maximum seven (7) years; all loans should be resolved (worked out/rehabilitated and turned over to the banks) well within that period.

- FINSAC must as a priority, recoup costs associated with collection of debts.

These guiding principles were then used to develop standard policies to ensure fair and uniform treatment of all debtors. A credit committee generally conducted case reviews, but the full board could be required to pass resolution on matters deemed to be beyond the competence of the credit committee. Standard policies applied to the following:

- Debt consolidation

- Decision authority

- Selection of workout strategy (including referrals to the oversight committee)

- Write-offs and relief (loan forgiveness, payment moratoriums)

- Finance (interest rates, extended payment tenure, accelerated repayments, payment allocation, miscellaneous fees/charges)

- Legal

- External service providers

- Asset repossession and realization

Debt Consolidation:

All common debt across the FINSAC portfolio was consolidated for workout purposes. Loan facilities sharing the same primary debtor(s) were treated as a single case. All debt settlement proposals had to address the liabilities in their entirety. FINSAC purchased non-performing loans from several banks. The reality of one client/borrower with non-performing loans at different institutions, as discussed earlier, became an issue that required a clear policy.

Decision Authority:

Decisions would require judgment on the part of the loan recovery unit. Decision rights were distributed across the FINSAC board, the credit committee, the loan recovery unit head, and loan recovery unit team managers. For decisions involving the compromise of a debt, the following terms were applied:

- **Write-off:** a compromise relative to the purchase price

- **Forgiveness:** a compromise on the balance outstanding, but in excess of the purchase price

The FINSAC board retained ultimate decision-making authority for the loan recovery unit's workout activities. The board reviewed decisions taken by the credit committee to ensure consistency with the agreed standard policies.

Selection of Workout Strategy:

All proposals were valued on a net present value (NPV) basis for the purpose of comparison—proposals with the highest NPV were usually recommended. Proposals falling below the highest were considered in instances where they were close to the NPV and the likelihood of success of the highest-ranked NPV proposal was low. Another factor that influenced the decision was whether the debtor's business operated in one of the productive sectors (e.g., manufacturing, agriculture, tourism). In such cases referral to the oversight committee set up by the government had to be considered, and the debtor, informed. During consideration by the oversight committee, the debtor could be permitted a moratorium on principal and interest (within the standard policy). Upon expiry of the moratorium, if the oversight committee indicated an inability to assist the debtor, FINSAC then acted unilaterally to inform and, if no further workable proposals emerged, to take its chosen course of action.

Write-offs and Relief:

No loan forgiveness could be approved prior to a debtor making either a significant lump-sum payment or consistent payments over a twelve-month period. In such cases, the credit committee approved the amount of loan forgiveness after reviewing written evidence of inability to repay the amount for which forgiveness was being sought. Payment moratoriums were allowed if performance under all terms of the repayment agreement between FINSAC, the debtor, and any third party lender (e.g., the National Investment Bank of Jamaica (NIBJ) or the National Development Bank of Jamaica (NDB), etc.) were agreed in accordance with the third party's submission.

Finance: Interest Rates, Extended Payment Tenure, Accelerated Repayments, Payment Allocation, and Miscellaneous Fees/Charges:

All extended loan payments accrued interest of at least 25% per annum on Jamaican dollar denominated loans and 15% per annum on U.S. dollar denominated loans. This held in all cases unless it was clearly recognized that collection of accrued interest would be impossible. Interest was determined by computing on a simple interest formula, based on the principal balance outstanding. The rate applicable was variable and loosely tied to the Treasury bill rate. These terms were significantly less onerous than those available from commercial banks. All costs associated with discharging debt and securities, including documentation charges, stamp duties, and transfer taxes, were added to debtors' accounts. Payments were allocated first to fees and charges, thereafter to principal, and only thereafter to interest. Payments received earlier than agreed were applied to principal. In cases extended payments were granted, up to a six-year maximum, where the proposed "new" payment schedule had an equivalent NPV to the original loan. Pledged securities were not released except in exchange for cash value of the security or for credit committee-approved security of higher value. FINSAC would not release securities for further interest to be noted thereon unless a reasonable payment arising from the additional liability of the debtor was forthcoming.

Legal:

All new agreements required that a standard legal contract be executed by the debtor, inclusive of the following clauses:

- Stated penalties for violation of contract terms

- Increased securitisation of debt

- Agreement to provide financial statements (including cash flow projections) and statement of affairs on an ongoing basis until the debt is expunged

- Statements must be provided within thirty days of the end of the accounting period

External Service Providers:

FINSAC established a list of approved service providers (real estate valuators and brokers, receivers, etc.) on the following basis:

- External valuators were retained on a flat-fee basis (based on type of real estate being valued).

- Receivers agreed to perform comprehensive situation diagnostic, including strategic options and recommendations, as well as to provide monthly audited financial statements/receiver's reports to FINSAC.

Asset Repossession and Realization:

- Assets were repossessed in instances of inadequate servicing of the liability with no feasible settlement proposal forthcoming.

- All assets divested via private treaty were handled by FINSAC's asset disposal unit.

- Attendant costs of seizure, storage, sale, etc., were recovered from sale proceeds of the asset.

- The seized asset(s) was/were sold at prices guided by professional valuations not older than six months in the case of motor vehicles and twelve months in the case of real estate.

- All real estate was first offered for sale by public auction before being referred for sale by private treaty. All properties available for sale by private treaty were listed with approved brokers; all such sales were subject to approval or ratification by the FINSAC board.

- Seizure of an asset did not relieve the debtor's obligations under the existing indebtedness; interest continued to accrue until the asset's divestment.

4

Protecting the Insured: Moral Hazard in Practice

The distressed institutions in the insurance industry were Crown Eagle Life Insurance Company, Dyoll Life Insurance Company, First Life Insurance Company, Island Life Insurance Company, Jamaica Mutual Life Assurance Society, and Life of Jamaica. They all prepared rehabilitation plans of their own in an approach to FINSAC for assistance. In varying degrees, their proposals for future viability were, for all but one, overly optimistic. If their assessment of the need for an immediate capital injection was of the order of $300 million to begin with, it was more likely at the end of the day to be of the order of $1 billion.

Lack of knowledge as to the true condition of a distressed business on the part of owners and managers is not by any means an unknown phenomenon in periods of crisis. On the contrary, it is well-known among lenders and financiers. Part of the cost of the rehabilitation exercise revolves around this very problem. Accountants, actuarial and insolvency experts, and other professionals, both locally and overseas based, had to be retained by FINSAC to determine the extent of insolvency and the most appropriate mechanisms for FINSAC assistance. It was the latter that proved a more difficult issue and sticking point. Two elements of the problem were the previously mentioned nature of the institutions—their interconnectedness and group structure—and in some cases, the attitude of the principals themselves.

FINSAC, having agreed to take control of an insolvent institution, first had to establish its legal ownership. This was not always as simple a task as one might presume. In one particular case, two integral members of a group had subscribed to the issued shares of a holding company. By forms of "Declaration of Trust," they declared these shares were held in trust for the relevant shareholders of the group's merchant bank. The reason for using this legal device was to allow the bank's shareholders to own the group's loss-making subsidiaries without the attendant negative effect this would have upon the financial position of the bank. The bank was, under the existing legislation in force, subject to regulatory inspection and monitoring. Effectively, this shareholding in trust would avoid the bank's having to show its financial position as linked to a member of a group with distressed subsidiaries—a financial condition disallowed by the law governing its operation. The bank's true financial position was thus effectively hidden from regulators.

These shares were to be transferred to the bank's owners upon attainment of positive net worth by the holding company. Up until the crash, this eventuality never did occur. In this case the consensus legal opinion held that the trust was void, having no legal effect because of its doubtful rationale in law. Furthermore, it was likely that there were no beneficiaries under the trust. In addition, there was ambiguity with respect to the trust's duration or indeed whether it would ever take effect—the trust was boundless in time. Thus FINSAC acquired ownership of the entire group by share transfer from the two individuals. The solution was simple, but its simplicity was by no means immediately self-evident. This situation is described in detail both to illustrate the type of problems faced during the task of rehabilitation and to indicate the point alluded to earlier: that periods of innovation created by taking advantage of legal "loopholes" in regulatory systems often precede financial crises.

The other general type of problem in this regard was that of some principals' attitudes to the resolution process. It was fairly well accepted by speculation that there would be a general election in 1997. Indeed, because of the sensitive nature of the matters being negotiated, both political parties agreed to keep FINSAC out of election campaign issues. Negotiations between FINSAC and a distressed entity would come to an amicable, mutually agreed closure. Commitment would be agreed, leaving only the legal paperwork to be done—in effect, a memorandum of understanding for signature before the agreement would take effect. The principals of the troubled institution would then attempt to bypass the mutual commitment by appealing directly to the Finance Minister or the Prime Minister in an attempt to delay an outcome they thought, or at least hoped, was not necessarily inevitable. In other words, what was really an economic, financial, accounting, and legal matter was being diverted into the political arena. Attempts at influence peddling were being taken to a different level. In cases, the tone of particular communications to the political directorate suggested blackmail. For instance, a letter might contain a preamble agreeing that Government could not allow systemic collapse, particularly since it had made a commitment to protect the institution's affected clientele. The second part of the communication might then indicate that agreement had to be reached before assistance could be set on stream to avoid open and public knowledge of the existing collapse. Pointing out that annual reports had to be published, otherwise the company would be delisted by the Jamaica Stock Exchange, it would then go on to suggest that such an eventuality would feed speculation and destroy confidence. The punch line would be that government should settle quickly, avoiding tortuous details and procedures upon which FINSAC was—from the viewpoint of the principals of the very institution that had become insolvent upon their watch—"unwisely" insisting.

Another type of response was to argue that government pledged to assist the institutions, in effect, to rescue shareholders and principals. Yet FINSAC was attempting to take away from principals the companies that they had built with so much sweat through difficult times. FINSAC, according to this view, was not acting in accordance with stipulated government policy. Furthermore, insistence on a holding of 26.5% of the ordinary shares of a distressed company as a requirement for injection of capital to make an institution solvent and viable was deemed direct evidence of the underhand attempt to take control or acquire the company as a matter of policy.

The position in law on the issue of protecting FINSAC's interest (the interest of the taxpayer) held that the minimum shareholding that would allow a challenge to majority shareholders in the event of attempts to vary the agreement of workout plans had to be 26.5%. Generally, the state of the institutions' financials, their insolvency, was so dire, that the value of the rescue capital injection required was much greater than 26.5% ordinary shareholding could achieve. In such cases preference shares were used to make up the difference, with specific conditions attached to their redemption. The responses of some principals were perverse, to say the least. They suggested that FINSAC should rescue the institution—as opposed to the stated policy of protecting depositors, pension funds, and the insured, in effect, the clients' assets—leaving its ownership and control structure absolutely unchanged. It was as if someone had squandered the inheritance—the farm was now under threat, bankrupt. Uncle comes to the rescue, pays off anxious, uneasy, and restive creditors and simply reaffirms the right of the nephew to continue harmful farming practices that could only, once again, destroy the enterprise.

Another variant of the response was to insist that the 26.5% shareholding should, by right of first refusal, be offered to the existing owners on some predetermined formula. In effect this would mean that an insolvent company, once rehabilitated, would be given back to its "owners." A bankrupt company has negative net worth. It owes more money than it can pay. In reality it has crashed. In the normal run of things, it would fold and be no more. FINSAC keeps it afloat at taxpayer's expense, in order to protect its clients. Such a procedure would mean that once the shares reached a positive value, there would be no sharing of the gain with the taxpayers who enabled the FINSAC capital injection in the first place—the result of such an agreement would have been a true owners' bailout. Such a procedure would have effectively rewarded non-performance, negligence, incompetence, and at worst, potentially criminal behaviours.

THE CONDITION OF THE INSURANCE INDUSTRY

Insurance companies' operations in Jamaica included both life and general insurance coverage. In 1996, the companies held within their operations approximately $17 billion of managed pension funds, $37 billion of life insurance, and $10 billion of general insurance (see Appendix B). The life insurance industry had experienced, and was continuing to experience, liquidity problems and reduced profitability; indeed, they were incurring losses. If this condition continued unchecked, insolvency would be the result; and in cases where it had already set in, it would worsen and further erode confidence in the financial services sector. At the time, the industry's spokespersons minimized the problems and viewed it simply as one of a liquidity crunch. Over the years it had become popular to create new insurance "products" that contained a minimum of insurance cover with an investment component that benefited from existing income tax provisions.

Because the companies were in cases also linked to unit trusts within the group, were engaged in significant real estate development in their own account—building head offices, shopping centres, purchasing land in areas presumed to be future prime sites for commercial purposes, and the like—and were, as well, investing in commercial real estate and major hotel properties, their asset portfolios were highly skewed toward the longer-term holdings, particularly, their real estate holdings. Encashment of policies designed for tax avoidance placed considerable stress on liquidity. To accommodate this development, which added to the problems of an underperforming real estate portfolio, the immediate solution was short-term loan instruments—commercial paper, often in the form of promissory notes, which were attractive to "depositors" for not being subject to income tax deduction at source. This in a period of rising interest rates was quite high-cost money. More alarmingly, some of the companies resorted to writing more of their new deposit-like products with a minimum of insurance cover.

By the time FINSAC intervened in the sector and had its first financial statements approved, covering its operations from incorporation date, January 29, 1997, to March 31, 1998, it had loans to financial institutions and investments totaling in excess of $19 billion. Assistance to the insurance subsector accounted for much of this figure. In order to assist the companies, FINSAC either made loans or acquired the company (or its subsidiaries, in whole or in part). By March 1998 the picture of FINSAC's subsidiary and associated companies looked like this:

Company Name	*FINSAC % Holding*
Eagle Group of Companies	86.0
Citizens Bank Ltd.	100.0
Refin Trust Ltd.	100.0
Recon Trust Ltd.	100.0
CIBC Jamaica Ltd.	25.0
NCB Jamaica Ltd.	40.0
NCB Group Ltd.	43.8
Island Life Insurance Co. Ltd.	26.5
Dyoll Group Ltd.	26.5
Life of Jamaica Ltd.	26.5
Billy Craig Finance and Merchant Bank Ltd.	49.0

Source: FINSAC Ltd. Auditors Report and Financial Statements, Period from date of incorporation January 29, 1997, to March 31, 1998, Deloitte & Touche, Kingston.

These holdings require some explanation. The Eagle Group was quickly realized to be insolvent and purchased for $1. Citizens Bank Ltd. and Canadian Imperial Bank of Commerce (CIBC) shares were acquired from Life of Jamaica in order to improve the condition of the company's core insurance operations.

In the 1990s Life of Jamaica had become the chief element in a local conglomerate that, its leaders suggested, would be among the Fortune 500 within a decade. This organization fit completely the description of what we described in our introduction as a "financial stable." Their strategy was to grow by acquisition and merger where possible—this strategy accounted for its considerable holdings in CIBC. FINSAC would provide a capital injection to the company to the value of 26.5% of its share capital; this, however, was insufficient to solve its problems. Thus Citizens Bank Ltd. and their holdings of 25% of the shares of the Canadian Imperial Bank of Commerce (CIBC) were also acquired. At the time of their haemorrhage, they were forced to consider sale of both these assets. Refin Trust Ltd. and Recon Trust Ltd. were companies created by FINSAC to hold the non-performing loans purchased from Citizens Bank Ltd. and National Commercial Bank (NCB)—a value that would exceed the $20 billion mark.

National Commercial Bank and NCB Group Ltd. were essentially part of the assets of the organization that grew out of government's purchase of Barclays Bank in the mid-1970s. Prevailing wisdom indicated the need for a group structure—the stable. In order for FINSAC to achieve its rescue of depositors, it would have to make injections that would clean up the bank's asset portfolio by taking out in excess of $19 billion in non-performing loans in the intervention phase. The complicated ownership and control structure dictated these purchases by FINSAC.

Island Life Insurance Company and Dyoll Group Ltd. were, at the time, a little less complicated. Dyoll had seen its competitors go into a variety of non-core businesses as well as create impressive head offices. In order to stay competitive in the future, Dyoll's management felt it could not be left out of the scramble for value. Dyoll therefore entered into arrangements which caused it to acquire a significant property holding for development and entry into the fields of tourism and coffee production. These ill-fated investments were draining the company. Island Life for its part had transformed more than $1 billion in cash into a head office and commercial real estate property that was—at arm's length—less than 50% occupied! The insurer itself occupied half of the building. Billy Craig Finance and Merchant Bank Ltd. was a company formed out of a thriving insurance brokerage firm that, like all the others, overreached and overextended itself. At the height of the crisis—June 30, 1996—when the companies had approached government for assistance to stave off a liquidity crisis and insolvency, the situation was assessed by FINSAC. Given the FINSAC mandate, this was of course necessary in order to determine the most effective mechanisms for support in an effort to protect the insured. Most of the accounts reviewed here relate to the periods ending between June and August of 1996.

THE COMPANIES

Crowne Eagle Life Insurance Company

Crown Eagle Life Insurance Company was thought to be one of the jewels in the crown of the Eagle Financial Network. The group boasted in excess of 60 companies. Several of these might best be described as dormant vehicles, existing to take advantage of probable developments too speculative to even venture a prediction. Apart from its insurance business, its active operations consisted basically of commercial banking, hotel and tourism real estate holdings, managed funds, and speculative real estate holdings (see Appendix C). Accounts for June 30, 1996, showed Crown Eagle Life Insurance Company holding 85% of its total assets in real estate and other investments unrelated to its insurance operations as follows:

	$ Million
Eagle Premium Growth Fund (EPGF)	6,631.06
Loan—EHIL[a]: Transfer of Real Estate and Equity from CEL	3,147.38
Interest in Subsidiaries Associated Companies	82.17
Equity	104.24
Real Estate	32.41
Total	9,997.26

*   Note a: Eagle Holdings & Investments Ltd.

Crown Eagle's associated short-term liabilities totaled $10,513.64 million, falling due within the 30- to 90-day period common for such loans. Interest costs associated with these loans hovered in the region of an average of 35%. They were made up as follows:

	$ Million
Bank Overdraft	386.55
Promissory Notes	7,458.09
Asset Investor	2,669.00
Total	10,513.64

These numbers and the relationships they represented presented almost insurmountable problems for the company. Yet the more immediate and particularly troubling feature of the company's operations was its very thin cash and liquid assets holdings coupled with the fact that, whereas it's 1996 financial statements reflected a reported loss of $371.16 million, removal of extraordinary income from capital gains ($851.50 million) and revaluation of the Eagle Premium Growth Fund ($751.06 million) would actually more than quintuple the reported loss figure to $1,973.82 million. Assets held in the group's growth fund included most of the offices (real estate) from which the group carried on its diverse operations. When the fund was first offered to the public, the buildings were acquired by connected operations within the group. Relying on the inflationary trends of the time, the book values were adjusted upward, leading to the fund's realization of both capital and revaluation gains. These forms of income—the result of accounting conventions—while appropriate in certain circumstances, would render the group's accounts attractive on appearance, but could contribute nothing beyond speculative projections for its future financial prospects.

Additionally, another negative result would have accompanied the device of revaluation of the Eagle Premium Growth Fund—it would have had a perverse effect. Quite contrarily to the hopes of Eagle's principals, revaluing the fund would certainly have caused unit holders, upon recognition that their holdings had appreciated, to seek encashment of some of their profits. The problem was that these "profits" were paper entries. The Eagle Group would therefore have had no liquidity to meet these demands.

Finally, at the height of the euphoric credit and real estate boom, the group embarked on construction of a set of luxury apartments in the upscale area of St. Andrew—Stony Hill. This magnificent structure on a promontory was billed as Kingston's soon-to-be most prestigious address. Takers there were, but how to fund it? Given the boom and inflation trends, projected costs continued escalating. In an effort to salvage the project, the concept was redesigned to create a hotel, thereby benefiting from the significant tax incentives available to the tourism sector. These gains on the one hand would simultaneously be accompanied by radical increases in construction costs. The building would eventually cost more than $1 billion to erect and represented a hotel which could never, in any foreseeable future, make a profit. Too far away from Kingston's business district, too hobbled by traffic gridlock to be a business-type hotel, and in no-man's-land relative to the tourist trade, this was really a pink elephant—literally and figuratively. No government policy could make correction for such ill-advised commitment of other people's money. Only a foolhardy subsidy would suffice. But on the horns of the dilemma of sunken capital and good money chasing that which was earlier ill-advisedly spent, the building had to be completed.[57]

The bubble had indeed burst. The prognosis was therefore that the company would face immediate cessation of its operations as further erosion of its capital base was unsustainable yet unavoidable.

Island Life Insurance Company

At June 30, 1996, Island Life Insurance Company held real estate to the value of $1,059 million, or 62.91% of the company's total investments. Return on real estate investment at this time was at an all-time low (in the region of less than 5%). Additionally, a major part of these holdings was tied to the company's new head office building—a commercial property erected, initially from of its own cash holdings, without binding prearranged leases and only partially tenanted. Finance costs gobbled up 28% of the company's income—equivalent to an amazing 45% of premium income! The picture was further darkened by the fact that its short-term liabilities of $468.95 million included $298.26 million of commercial paper with maturities from 30 to 90 days at an average interest rate of 35%. The balance would become due in two to three years. The company was actually experiencing negative cash flows. Island Life had joined the euphoria later than its competitors and had a smaller and less diverse group structure—five companies devolved to the hands of FINSAC. One of these was the Island Victoria Bank, a joint venture with the Victoria Mutual Building Society (see Appendix C).

Life of Jamaica

Life of Jamaica's real estate and other holdings unrelated to its core business stood at $4,163.20 million at July 31, 1996. This represented 72.69% of its total investments:

	$ Million
Real Estate	1,807.9
Hotel	602.1
Investments in Subsidiaries	1,172.0

	$ Million
Corporate Stocks (CIBC)	581.2
Total	4,163.2

Financing these long-term investments were external borrowings of $2,006 million, with commercial paper (of 30- to 90-days maturity) accounting for $1,485 million, or 74% of the total, at an average interest rate of 36.18%. The company had also supplemented its general fund by borrowing $907 million from its segregated funds. Long-term investments were being financed by short-term borrowings, raising the specter of a looming liquidity crisis. At July 1996, interest costs were of the order of $339.1 million, representing 21% of gross revenue.

Jamaica Mutual Life Assurance Society

At June 30, 1996, Jamaica Mutual Life Assurance Society held real estate and equity investments in associated companies of $6,628.33 million—over 70% of its total assets. These long-term investments were being financed by short-term deposits at rates in excess of 35%, creating a projected finance cost in 1996, at the time of FINSAC's assessment, of $1,733 million. Unable to generate revenues to cover these costs, the society had begun to increase its short-term borrowings simply to remain operational. It also increased its borrowings from its subsidiary, NCB, to more than double the bank's capital base. Both National Commercial Bank and Mutual Security Bank were in the group owned by the society. The society's asset holdings were as follows:

	$ Million
Investment Property	3,069.51
Freehold Property	679.49
Investment in Subsidiaries	1,368.35
Investment in Associated Companies	1,510.98
Total	6,628.33

Short-term loans enabling interim financing of its operations amounted to $4,714.40 million, made up as follows:

	$ Million
Commercial Paper	435.0
Mutual Investor Plus	3,174.0
Mutual Security Bank	240.9
Staff and Administration	411.1
Current Portion of Long-term Loans	<u>435.4</u>
Total	4,714.4

These figures represented Mutual Life's accounts to August 1996. The portfolio of Commercial Paper would fall due within 90 days of the reporting date. $1,396 million, or 44%, of the Mutual Investor Plus policies would also fall due at the same time. Insolvency of the society was evident from its December 31, 1995 accounts, which indicated a deficiency in its Life Assurance and Annuity Fund in the amount of $2,500 million. The society had already crashed at the end of 1995. It was bleeding millions of dollars on a daily basis and had no way to avoid this. Whereas the Life Assurance and Annuity Fund stood at $3,500 million, the reserve required for future projected payout was $6,000 million. The problem was most acute and, as in the case of Crown Eagle Life Insurance Company, without a rescue package, its operations would be forced to close in face of both liquidity problems and outright insolvency. At the root of the society's distress was the collapse in value of both its real estate and other equity holdings—investments that accounted for over 70% of the society's total assets.

Dyoll Life Insurance Company

For all intents and purposes, Dyoll Life's difficulties could be traced to one real estate investment decision—a loan to developers for a tourism property development at Drax Hall. This deal fell through when the property developers were unable to complete financing arrangements for the project and the loan went sour. Dyoll acquired the property at a book value of $137.8 million, subsequently revalued to $466.2 million. The effect of this was to raise the real estate portion of its total investments to more than 80% at June 30, 1996. As with its sister insurance companies, short-term borrowing at high interest rates (in the region of 40%), coupled with non-performance of its real estate holding, added to the existing liquidity problems. Interest costs represented over 30% of both total revenue and premium income.

First Life Insurance Company

Compared to the liquidity and solvency problems of the other insurance companies previously described, First Life Insurance Company in 1996 faced minor problems. Approximately 70% of its total assets were held as investments in subsidiaries and associated companies. This in itself did not present the immediate potential for liquidity problems. The major potential issue was that of its real estate fund: if holders sought to encash their units, at a time (1996) when there was no prospect of significant increase in the near term, there could be liquidity problems. Short-term liabilities were in the region of $50 million, but the company held over $280 million in cash, other deposits, and Government of Jamaica securities. Their approach to FINSAC was therefore merely a step in pursuit of prudence. The prognosis for First Life was fair, and any assistance could be contemplated as likely to be minimal and of a relatively short duration.

INTERNAL SOLUTION EFFORTS

All the insurance companies attempted, albeit too late, to stem the tide of descent into insolvency. They implemented measures to reduce their agent commissions' structure, rationalize branch networks, and reduce administrative costs. The companies in the initial stages were generally either reluctant or unwilling to divest themselves of non-core businesses that would ultimately improve their positions. In addition, when they approached government, the idea was for mounting a "rescue package" for the group. While there is no fool-proof mechanism of verification, it does appear that the attitude of wanting to hold on to underperforming assets that either represented part of the perceived importance of the group or embodied a plank in the long-term strategy for growth of the group was one of the reasons they fell into difficulties in the first place.

However, it should be noted that in the climate of the mid-1990s, when the crunch had actually set in, it would have been quite difficult, if not impossible, to dispose of some of these assets on favourable terms. Yet from the beginning of negotiations, the companies wanted to hold on to their real estate, banks, and equities held in the group structure, even in the face of impending or actual insolvency. In actuality, the companies expected support of the government by taxpayer funds, while their unsound operations remained fundamentally unchanged. In light of the fact that taxpayer dollars would have to be spent and the management cultures of the flailing organizations would remain in tact, this was hardly a scenario that could have been acceptable to government.

FINSAC: INTERVENTION AND REHABILITATION

In most cases the insurance companies participated in, owned, or controlled banks. In others, banks existed in the same group that owned, or controlled insurance companies. These relationships made it easy to arrange overdraft and loan accommodations to the companies. Inappropriateness of this relationship was early recognized, and rehabilitation would end them. Rehabilitation would also require issuance of lump-sum policies to be discontinued and the existing ones paid out. The companies had resorted to issuing more of these policies in a perversely misguided effort to raise immediate cash to meet policyholders' withdrawals from existing policies. They were "borrowing from Peter to pay Paul"!

FINSAC's diagnostic review of the distressed companies identified the following features which had to be addressed:

- Overinvestment in real estate

- Extremely low overall returns on investment

- Too high surrender rates due to the deposit-like nature of the new insurance products

- Guaranteed rates of return on interest-sensitive policies of between 12%–24% were unsustainable and imprudent

- Too high commission levels for new business

- Little or no incentives for renewal business

- Too high levels of expenses, significantly above international industry norms

- Highly leveraged operations

- Difficulty in meeting solvency requirements

These difficulties derived from several factors, among which was the rush for growth as group conglomerates without either sufficient capital or necessary expertise to manage non-core businesses. This objective led the companies to compete aggressively. The practice of "stealing" top-performing agents became common. To achieve this, the companies had to pay high commissions. To write new business in cutthroat competition, the sales force ignored the appropriateness of policies for clients, and surrender rates climbed. Lump-sum policies were quasi insurance products, allowable under the prevailing regulations and made more attractive by the existing tax regime. They were inappropriate to the core business of the insurance industry and proved to be a major factor contributing to its liquidity problems and resultant lack of viability.

Initially, the strategy contemplated by FINSAC was to restructure and merge the portfolios of failed companies into an entirely new company prior to ultimate divestment. This initial decision was revised after consideration of the significant expense that would be involved in creating and operating a new company from scratch. The alternate strategy chosen would be less costly and relied on accelerated divestment in which the insurance portfolios were sold by invitation to tender.

That decision taken, it was imperative that the lump-sum, interest-sensitive policies be excised from the companies' portfolios. Although this option would require immediate funding, inclusion of these policies, with their debilitating costs, would render the whole portfolio unattractive to potential buyers. In more than 90% of lump-sum, interest-sensitive policies held in the industry, the policyholder's life was insured for $60,000 or less, as compared to an average coverage in the range of $250,000 for the more normal savings-type interest-sensitive policies of the industry as a whole. Inclusion of these would certainly have made the portfolios impossible to sell except at a true fire-sale markdown. The new strategy proved effective. Eight companies from Jamaica and the wider Caribbean responded to the invitation for bids published by FINSAC.

To remove lump-sum policies from the portfolios, FINSAC negotiated and funded a scheme with the Bank of Nova Scotia Jamaica Ltd. In which holders of lump-sum, interest-sensitive policies would be repaid all their investment in these types of policy. The benefit for Scotiabank was that it would have access to a potentially new customer base without the normally associated marketing costs. The idea was to fulfill government's pledge to protect the insured. The population most at risk, the holders of "small" policies—actually 78.8% of all policyholders—would immediately receive all their moneys. They simply had to access an account opened for them with Scotiabank. The other 21.2% would immediately be repaid up to $200,000 in cash, with the balance being repaid later.

Cash to a limit of $200,000 was paid into an account opened in each policyholder's name at the Bank of Nova Scotia. For the 21.2% of policyholders with over $200,000 held in lump-sum, interest-sensitive policies, the balance of their funds was placed in a Scotia Trust 7-year Certificate of Participation with the following terms:

• Tax-free interest paid twice per year at BNS passbook rate

• Principal would not be available prior to maturity in 7 years

• Certificates were tradable and could be used as collateral

With this scheme FINSAC set out to provide the rescue implied in government's pledge to those most in need—small savers in the economy. But as appropriate and considerate as it appeared, this scheme was not good enough.

As a practical matter, quite a large number of pensioners were affected by the fallout in the insurance sector. As provision for retirement, many had invested their pensions and/or other savings accumulated for security in old age. Completely unexpectedly, they found themselves unable to cover day-to-day living expenses. In special consideration of their plight, the Ministry of Finance decided to vary the terms such that pensioners 65 years or older at March 31, 1999, would receive monthly interest payments. This would allow them to meet their expenses on a timely basis until their certificates of participation matured. Subsequently, resulting from the provisions of another initiative, government decided to reduce the maturity period on the certificates of participation from 7 to 5 years. In the 1999 budget, government created a new 5-year savings instrument allowing tax-free interest earnings once the principal was left untouched. Having provided this benefit for some, equity required changing the maturity on the certificates already issued.

The next step in the process required court appointment of a Judicial Manager to oversee management and sale of the insurance portfolios of the companies—Crown Eagle, Dyoll Life, and Mutual Life. The Judicial Manager would be responsible for filing a report with the court, stating which of the available options was in the best interest of policyholders. The report was filed with the superintendent of insurance and was made available for public scrutiny. Once a court order was received, the decision of the court was binding on all persons. In April of 1999, the Judicial Manager filed the report with the Supreme Court regarding the lump-sum, interest-sensitive policies. The court ruled that the FINSAC-pioneered scheme to pay out these policies formerly marketed by Crown Eagle, Mutual Life, and Dyoll Life was the best deal possible for policyholders.

At March 1999, the FINSAC/Bank of Nova Scotia/Bank of Nova Scotia Trust Initiative had been accessed by 4,091 policyholders, with a total liability of $2.5 billion. For U.S. dollar denominated policies, 11 policyholders had taken advantage of the scheme, with a total liability of US$334,000. The combined figures represented 52% of all policyholders and 80% of the total liabilities. As an interim measure, FINSAC provided an emergency fund facility, allowing policyholders who could establish hardship and extreme need to obtain advance funds from their policies. A total of $32,733,861.77 was advanced to 2,514 policyholders under the programme.

For those policy holders who did not accept or wish to participate in the scheme, the Supreme Court agreed that lump-sum, interest-sensitive policies should be transferred to Larnaka Limited, a subsidiary created by FINSAC for this express purpose. Policies held by Lanarka were transferred to Guardian Life if their value was under $200,000 or to Union Bank if greater than $200,000. U.S. dollar policies were to be paid out.

5

Banking Interventions

All the indigenous commercial and merchant banks were overburdened with bad loans. When they approached FINSAC, their in-house assessment of this inert portfolio was too optimistic. It is a kind of reactive mechanism—a process of denial. Without fail, the true picture of loans that had to be taken over by FIN-SAC ended up a larger value than was first represented. The banks affected were eight all told:

- Citizens Bank Limited

- Citizens Merchant Bank Limited

- Corporate Merchant Bank Limited

- Eagle Commercial Bank Limited

- Island Life Merchant Bank

- Island Victoria Bank Limited

- National Commercial Bank

- Workers Savings & Loan Bank

In attempting both to understand the details of the banks' distress and to devise a workable solution, the process was never as smooth as this narrative might suggest. Individual banks approached FINSAC at different times. Their estimates of needed support were themselves never bankable. Their ownership structures presented problems, and various legal devices had to be used to effect the changes ultimately decided upon. For the flow of the narrative, we treat National Commercial Bank separately from the others simply because of the merger process which created one bank, fusing all the others into a new entity—Union Bank.

National Commercial Bank

In 1977 the British Barclays Bank sold Barclays Bank Jamaica Ltd. to the government. It was renamed National Commercial Bank. Early in the 1980s, government divested approximately 51% of its shares in NCB. In 1986, in keeping with the prevailing vision of the usefulness and superiority of the group structure we discussed earlier, NCB's shareholders and management took the decision to create a new entity—NCB Group Limited. National Commercial Bank Jamaica Limited became a fully owned subsidiary of NCB Group Limited, with the shareholders of the Bank receiving shares in NCB Group Limited by means of a share swap. Subsidiaries of the National Commercial Bank Jamaica Limited also became subsidiaries of NCB Group by the same process.

In a government divestment of its residual shareholding, Jamaica Mutual Life Assurance Society and Jamaica National Building Society created a joint venture company, JM&N, to purchase government's interest in the NCB Group. Although NCB Group was listed on the Stock Exchange and was widely held, the size of this transaction gave JM&N effective control of NCB Group Limited—this of course was the specific intent of the joint venture of the two societies.

The circumstances immediately prior to and surrounding this transaction are interesting and provide some insight into subsequent events. The sale occurred at a time when both government revenues and foreign exchange holdings were under stress. Divestment was thus both a reflection of the new privatization policy thrust and a revenue-enhancing mechanism. There were some who opposed the idea on three grounds. A pledge had been made to the Jamaican people that, when government was divesting its 49% shareholding in the bank, public participation would be allowed. Existing shareholders would have the right of first refusal, subject of course to the shareholding limitation of 10% total holding. Secondly, the joint venture company, while it clearly could afford the purchase price of the transaction, did not seem to have the adequate capital backing necessary for such a large acquisition. Finally, the sale would overly concentrate power in the small Jamaican society, and the expertise did not exist in the combined organization to manage a conglomerate of the size, scope, and diversity to be created.

The management team at Mutual Life was perhaps too narrowly concentrated in the insurance business. Yet, as with so many other aspects of prevailing orthodoxy in the Jamaican corporate schema, the expertly created public relations hype suggested otherwise. The team at NCB did not itself appear to bring the levels of expertise necessary to render the merged entity competent. For many years before the acquisition, the effective controllers of the bank had been its management team. They embarked on a process of promotion from within. They moved into ventures in which they had little expertise. Everyone in the top management team had come through the ranks of Barclays/NCB. The probability that all the requisite skills would be found in-house for a group that was now engaged in such diverse activities is perhaps zero! In nature there is the ever-present need for mechanisms that promote and guarantee genetic diversity and strength. At NCB no such mechanisms seem to have existed. Some suggested that, what is called in Jamaica, the "buddy syndrome" prevailed. Reports of young graduates hired by the bank suggested that new recruits with fresh ideas were regarded as threatening to the existing power structure and were summarily informed that they must either play the running game or face a time-out call.

The managing group, as suggested by some critics on talk shows and elsewhere, evidently threw away Barclays' manuals covering prudential management and conflict of interest. The fact that the bank embarked heavily on non-core, non-banking activities meant that, inevitably, the "bank" would end up in competition with its customers. But additionally, it was alleged that NCB executives would steal a client's idea after turning down a loan. These executives, as the story wafted abroad, owned or participated in ownership of diverse businesses—car rental companies, hotels, apartments, farms, used-car dealerships, etc. Junior members of staff were alleged to be disgruntled at the way in which executives could flout guidelines with respect to loans, which they could have at subsidized rates, apparently devoid of any notion of conflict of interest. Certainly this picture could not be a reflection of the whole management team. Yet many clients, former clients, rejected potential borrowers, and employees holding these allegations to be true never initiated any proceedings for redress. No one, as far as the author can discern, has ever been willing to go on the record with such claims.

These features associated with NCB were not thought to be isolated. If such a management atmosphere did indeed exist, the perilous state of the bank's assets would not strike even the most casual observer as surprising. Be that as it may, in such an environment, the diluted shareholding of less than 10% that government had originally pledged, while beautiful and egalitarian in the abstract, in practice would not prove to be a good idea. Such a scheme would merely have enhanced the stranglehold the management team had over the bank's path, moving its strategy and culture into the future. While this may have been one of the factors taken into account in the process of decision making in the divestment, that there may have been influence peddling in the choice among an array of options regarding divestment cannot be ruled out. That the array of options was never really an array at all is also a distinct possibility!

As a result of its disproportionate volume of non-performing loans to arm's-length clients, failed ventures of the group's non-core activities, and loan accommodation to one of its primary parents, Jamaica Mutual Life Assurance Society, NCB Group and the bank suffered significant losses and erosion of their capital base. Mutual Life, during its period of haemorrhage to lump-sum, interest-sensitive policies and poorly performing real estate ventures, had overburdened its already distressed banking subsidiary.

FINSAC, through the negotiation and intervention process, acquired their non-performing loans—replacing these assets with FINSAC notes, convertible into cash under certain circumstances. This loan purchase had the effect of providing liquidity support and recapitalization for a total of $19.5 billion. $13.5 billion purchased non-performing loans or bad debts while $6 billion purchased a mix of ordinary and preference shares on the 26.5% basis already discussed. The FINSAC support translated into acquisition of 40% of the outstanding ordinary shares of NCB from NCB Group Limited and 43.8% of NCB Group Limited, making it the single largest shareholder in NCB Group. FINSAC named six members to the board of directors.

A precondition for support required the bank to develop a rehabilitation plan to be approved by FINSAC. This plan was augmented with input from FINSAC's consultants and monitored on an ongoing basis. Among the conditions of FINSAC assistance was the requirement that net profit after tax had to be retained in the NCB banking reserve fund in order to achieve and maintain a minimum primary capital base to total assets ratio of 8%, and a minimum capital base to risk weighted assets ratio of 12%. In addition, the bank and the group had to divest themselves of non-core business in order to concentrate on banking and financial services—their primary activity. NCB Group Limited had significant investments in real estate, agriculture, and tourism—some twenty-five subsidiaries (see Appendix C).

The restructured NCB Group quickly moved from a loss of $1 billion in 1998 to a net profit of $405 million for the year ended September 1999. Of course the major contributor to this turn around was its holdings of FINSAC paper in place of its bad debts—FINSAC paper, government backed bonds paid 1% above the

Treasury bill-weighted average interest rate. The arrangements for these interest payments were semiannual, either in cash or bonds, depending on the needs of the bank and the exigencies of prevailing monetary policy. But there were other changes mandated by the rehabilitation plan. The bank had to rationalize its branch network. Prior to the purchase of NCB by JM&N, the Jamaica Mutual Life Assurance Society had acquired the former Royal Bank of Canada that operated in Jamaica, renaming it Mutual Security Bank. The JM&N acquisition of NCB meant absorbing Mutual Security Bank. The branches of the merged group's banks were sometimes a mere thirty metres apart—on the opposite sides of the same road. The plan also called for rationalization of staff.

FINSAC employed the services of the highly regarded Hong Kong and Shanghai Banking Corporation (HSBC) to prepare the bank for eventual divestment of its stake in NCB and NCB Group.

UNION BANK: CITIZENS, EAGLE, ISLAND VICTORIA, WORKERS

Citizens Bank Limited, Citizens Merchant Bank Limited, Corporate Merchant Bank Limited, Eagle Commercial Bank Limited, Island Life Merchant Bank, Island Victoria Bank Limited, and Workers Savings & Loan Bank all required FINSAC support. They were merged primarily for reasons of scale and efficiencies. Independently, each of the banks would have proven neither viable nor attractive to prospective buyers. Merged, however, the banks would maximize both market presence and customer retention. Additionally, merged into one unit, the resultant bank would benefit from distinct cost reductions associated with scale of operation for a variety of reasons. Globally, in the year 2000 (Y2K) anxieties were uppermost in the minds of participants in the financial sector. Using a common technology, Y2K compliance requirements coupled with the relevant replacement costs would be minimized for one bank. Finally, merging the assets of all the banks would immediately improve their solvency and liquidity position. The merger consolidated a branch network of forty-one branches to twenty-one, located island-wide, with representation in most major towns.

Union Bank of Jamaica Limited became the third largest bank on the island, with total assets of $33.85 billion, a loan portfolio of $1.27 billion, and deposit liabilities of $17.8 billion at the end of 2000. Initially the business of Island Victoria Bank, Eagle Commercial Bank, and Workers Savings and Loan Bank was consolidated under FINSAC. Inclusion of Citizens Bank as part of Union Bank occurred subsequently.[58] Shareholders then voted at Citizens Bank's 1999 Annual General Meeting to change the name of Citizens Bank to Union Bank of Jamaica. That meeting also authorized the injection of over $2 billion of new capital by FINSAC into the bank. This increased FINSAC's stake in the bank to 99.4% from the 60% stake initially acquired from Life of Jamaica in 1997 as part of the package of financial assistance provided to the ailing insurance company at that time.

Union Bank was sold to RBTT International Limited, a member of the RBTT Financial Group of Trinidad & Tobago, by an agreement with FINSAC in March 2001. To achieve this, a mandatory offer had to be made to the minority shareholders. The bank was renamed RBTT, replacing the newly named Union Bank of Jamaica.

6

Divestments

Selling the Portfolios of Crown Eagle, Dyoll, and Mutual Life

Upon the decision to combine and divest the insurance portfolios of Mutual Life Assurance Company, Crown Eagle Life Insurance Company, and Dyoll Life Insurance Company, tenders were invited.[59] FINSAC contacted all local and Caribbean companies thought potentially capable of absorbing the combined portfolio and invited them to bid. Nine companies indicated expressions of interest. Eight were allowed to enter the bidding process:

- Barbados Mutual Life Assurance Society

- Blue Cross of Jamaica

- Colonial Life Insurance Company (Trinidad) Ltd.

- First Life Insurance Company Ltd.

- Guardian Holdings Ltd.

- Life of Barbados Ltd.

- Maritime Life (Caribbean) Ltd.

- Prime Life Assurance Company Ltd.

Life of Barbados Ltd. and Barbados Mutual Life Assurance Society subsequently decided to bid for the portfolios as a joint venture.

THE BID PROCESS

FINSAC having accepted Memoranda of Understanding (loosely translated: documents outlining rules of engagement), bidders were informed of the bid process, related requirements, and submission deadlines. To make the portfolios more attractive, potential purchasers were allowed to bid for the portfolios either in whole or in part. They could also make their bids contingent on successful tender for other segments of the business. This would allow prospective purchasers to fit their new acquisition snugly into their existing operations. Another feature of the process allowed FINSAC to accept the offer for a portfolio made by one company or any combination of companies. Additionally, similar portfolios from the three companies were combined. This offered buyers specific lines of business, rather than the particular mix that the portfolios of the three companies happened to hold at the time of their demise. Bidders were not allowed to tender for the portfolio of just one of the failed companies. The major concern underlying the former decision was a preference for playing to the strengths, expertise, and core competencies of the bidding companies. In order to assess and make final judgement on the bids, each bid was allotted points based on how well they measured up against a set of ranking criteria. Bidders with the highest points standing would emerge winners.

VALUATION

Most important in this process was actuarial valuation of the portfolios. The portfolios were valued by type: individual life business; pension business; and group business—health and life. Upon completion, each actuarial valuation report was sent to bidders. The bidders in turn were then required to submit a bid for that particular portfolio. Valuation was based on policy and performance data provided by the three insurance companies as at December 31, 1998. But there were difficulties. The first hurdle in this valuation process was the fact that there was no standard accounting or actuarial practice governing the Jamaican insurance industry. The solution chosen was simple enough: two standard methods in common use internationally in the industry. The policy premium method (PPM) was chosen for valuation, and the related minimum continuing capital and surplus requirements (MCCSR), to establish the financial strength of the bidding companies.

There were also two existing factors favouring the methods chosen. The first was that use of both systems was highly likely to become mandated requirements of the projected new Insurance Act for Jamaica. Second, these methods were already being used by two Jamaican companies: First Life Insurance Company and Life of Jamaica. They were also being used by some companies in Barbados.

Policy Premium Method

The policy premium method is a means of calculating the actuarial liabilities of insurance companies. It indicates the minimum reserves respective companies should hold to meet obligations to policyholders. In deriving the liabilities, PPM makes assumptions as to mortality, lapse rates, administrative expenses, and interest rates (among other factors) for each policy type. The valuations took into account the specific experience of each company as well as assumptions appropriate to the Jamaican economy and society.

Minimum Continuing Capital and Surplus Requirements (MCCSR)

The minimum continuing capital and surplus requirements (MCCSR) uses the actuarial liabilities and asset mix to measure an insurer's capital adequacy to meet its obligations to policyholders. Simply put, this measure tries to determine the size of a "company's wallet" relative to its likely expenses. The MCCSR ratio is expressed as a percentage of the minimum requirement. In other words, a MCCSR of 100% means that a company has adequate capital to meet its obligations to policyholders.

Automatic Disqualifiers

Automatic disqualifiers established the potential owners' ability to meet the divestment committee's minimum requirements, including "fit and proper" considerations. Bidders were disqualified if any of the following requirements were not met:

- The company's MCCSR after acquisition should exceed 100%.

- There should be no reason to doubt that the affairs of the bidding entity were exercised with good corporate governance, due diligence, and in accordance with properly formulated plans and strategies.

- The directors/owners should not have been under indictment in proceedings of bankruptcy, fraud, customs violations, tax, or securities violations.

- The operating plan, business plan, annual reports, and other requested information were submitted.

- No bids would be taken from companies or subsidiaries of companies in which FINSAC had intervened. It would not be in the best interest of taxpayers for a company in which government had to mount a rescue effort to divert funds from their own rehabilitation process to buy other government-owned or controlled entities.

Once the bidder had cleared this phase, their bids moved forward to the evaluation process detailed in the following criteria:

Criterion 1: Financial Capacity

The potential owner should have had the financial capacity to acquire and operate the business, with MCCSR ratio of 100% for the consolidated entity being a passing score.

Areas Considered
The MCCSR ratios after acquisition were ranked in the following bands:

- 100%–109%

- 110%–119%

- 120%–129%

- 130%–139%

- 140%–149%

- 150% and greater

Adequacy of liquidity to support the acquisition in a balance sheet review also had to be established.

Criterion 2: Assessment of Historical Performance and Future Plans

Historical performance and business plans submitted had to demonstrate managerial capability specific to the industry.

Criterion 3: Bid Price

The bid price was ranked against that of other qualified bidders. Ranking was performed on the final bid for the entire portfolio. Where a company did not bid on the entire portfolio, it was first ranked within its group. The bidder attaining the highest point value was then grouped with a suitable partner or partners and ranked for the entire portfolio. The highest bid gained maximum points with one point deducted for every $10 million below the maximum submitted by lower bidders.

The results of the bid process were as follows:

• Group Life and Health: First Life Insurance Company Limited

• Pension and Annuities: Guardian Holdings

• Individual Life: Guardian Holdings

The bid price for the entire portfolio was $1,310.3 million. Guardian Holdings is a Trinidad and Tobago-based company; First Life Insurance Company Limited, a Jamaican company.

Assets amounting to $5.5 billion had to be transferred to the purchasers.[60] Of this amount $2 billion would be sourced from the existing assets of Mutual Life Assurance Society, Crown Eagle, Dyoll Life, and other companies acquired by FINSAC. Negotiations with the successful bidders determined the specific assets that were finally transferred. The remaining $3.5 billion would be provided by government debt instrument, a significant portion of which would be a ten-year or longer-term bond instrument. This was required because, even though the companies had real estate assets of value, they could not be transferred to the successful bidder, as it would leave the new owner with a portfolio too skewed toward real estate—one of the causes of the companies' problems in the first place. Indeed no prudent bidder would have accepted such a portfolio mix.

LIFE OF JAMAICA

Life of Jamaica was divested to Barbados Mutual for $2 billion. They merged the new acquisition with the original purchase of the portfolio of Island Life Insurance Company.

NCB

National Commercial Bank took a long time to come off the block. The HSBC deal did not yield more than lukewarm indications of interest. Eventually a deal was struck with the Canadian-based AIC Investment, which was headed by Jamaican born Michael Lee Chin. The sale price was $6.03 billion, payable on a schedule. At the time of sale in March 2002, $2,650,261,600 was paid. Thereafter the balance would be paid in eight annual installments of $422,977,018.75 each, to end on March 2010.

NON-PERFORMING LOANS

As a result of the decision to protect depositors, FINSAC acquired $32 billion in bad debts from the failed banks. Of this, the in-house collection unit achieved collections of $6.4 billion. The remainder of $25.6 billion was sold in February 2002, in a deal with the Jamaican Redevelopment Foundation Inc., a locally incorporated entity with Beal Bank of Texas as parent. The "foundation" then incorporated another entity, Denis Joslin Jamaica Inc., to manage the collections. The U.S. dollar equivalent of the bad debt was US$393 million. FINSAC struck an agreement in which US$23 million was paid up front. FINSAC would receive 15% of the next US$50 million collected, with the scale rising to 50% of collections from the 5th tranche of US$50 million.

While these terms may appear to the uninitiated to be a giveaway, the point is that collectibility of bad loans is always a murky affair. Bad loan purchasing is worse than buying junk bonds. The risk is high; the price must be sufficiently low to justify the investor's decision. There is never a queue waiting to purchase a bad loan portfolio in any market, much less in the so-called emerging markets. One outstanding element of the bad loan portfolio remained. $6.8 billion consisted of loans to government entities, partly government-owned entities, or entities that enjoyed government guarantees. If these loans were sold, it would mean government paying itself. These were to be written off the books of FINSAC if, at the end of the day, no change was likely or perceived.

7

Aftermath: Fiduciary Responsibility, Ethics in Business, Society's Gain vs. Loss

"[N]o matter how much effort is made to improve the legislative framework, and how much human and financial resources are devoted to strengthening the supervisory process, there will always be one essential element that is required, if the people of Jamaica are to have confidence in their financial system. **This element is integrity...not everyone in the financial system shares the same philosophy...some have a confused view of what is meant by fiduciary responsibility. They have exhibited a tendency to believe that depositors' money is their money and have in the process lent to them selves large sums of money to purchase real estate or other assets in pursuit of their own self-ambition.** They have repeatedly violated the law in full cognizance of it and quite **often they have been supported in their endeavours by some members of the legal and accounting profession.**"[61]

These comments of former governor of the Bank of Jamaica, Jacques Bussierres, in a speech to the Life Insurance Companies Association of Jamaica on March 8, 1996, are pertinent. Why he waited until his job was done, or more appropriately, until he was close to the end of his contract, to pronounce on these important matters is a bit of a mystery. These are issues that should have been addressed at commencement of his tour of duty, when his admittedly complex and decidedly delicate job had begun!

On the other hand, it might be firstly noted that he could not have immediately known of these behaviours. Secondly, once they became apparent, he appears to have worked behind the scenes to right the situation in order to avoid the immediate drain in confidence that exposure would have caused. In that endeavour, he obviously failed. Another issue contributing to his inability to transform the system should be raised here. It is the fact that some with fiduciary responsibility in the institutions appear genuinely to have had no understanding of the true workings of deposit-taking institutions in a financial system. Some actually believed that liquidity problems could be solved merely by going to London, Birmingham, Toronto, or New York, and encouraging Jamaican communities there to participate in deposit and investment schemes to prepare for their retirement and help build their country. In fact, by taking more deposits, they would have made their situation worse! Some high-level managers of the domestic institutions, once they moved beyond functions like marketing and public relations, were entirely out of their depth. When it came to critical technical issues of the financial enterprise, their PR agencies' creations were of very little use. But some seemed to have come to believe their own advertising copy.

Creation of groups does not automatically result in the contagion and ultimate crash that ensued. The economies of scale and synergies mentioned in our earlier discussion do exist. They embody significant avenues for a variety of cost savings that cannot be dismissed out of hand. The problem however is that the nature of the group structure requires of its top-level management even greater degrees of competence, personal confidence, independence, integrity, and knowledge of risk assessment techniques, financial system interactions, and the law. Furthermore, the boards of the various institutions within the group should be populated by individuals willing and able to exercise fiercely independent judgment, guided by the aforementioned qualities and competencies. Finally, the regulatory system and its executive personnel should be adequate for the task at hand. Whether Jamaica during this period possessed the capacity to provide such a cluster of skills is perhaps debatable. Whether those skills, even if identified, would have been deployed in the sector as they should have been, is doubtful. That the regulatory system was inadequate is beyond rational debate.

Yet if we look at the industrialized countries, taking the United States as our example, at the very time that FINSAC was seized of the view that sticking to core business was the preferred alternative, several institutions in the financial services industry were merging and creating conglomerates, as for instance, the CITIGROUP. Should we by assumption agree, although we should not, that Jamaica possessed the cluster of skills referred to previously, there are still some significant differences that exist between the Jamaican situation and that of the United States. First, the regulatory system is much more robust; breaches of regulations are thus more likely to be identified. Furthermore, penalties for breaches—white-collar crimes—are thought to be automatic. In addition, the legal system of the

United States, even though it does take a considerable time to arrive at decisions, is much more efficient in this area than that of Jamaica's. In other words, while recognizing that temptation will always exist, and that such temptation will be more intense where weakness is detected, remedies must exist and consequences for breaches should be expected to follow such occurrences as a matter of course. This was not the case in Jamaica.

Bear in mind that creation of the joint stock company during Britain's colonial expansion, and further refinement in its industrial revolution, was critical to both capitalism and its capacity to amalgamate capital for wealth creation. That mechanism has been improved and enhanced to levels of refinement and sophistication that were unthinkable then. Today the world's capital markets are mysterious to some, perhaps unbelievable to others. Stock exchanges and financial systems of the world, however, can operate only to the extent that their participants trust the validity of information being provided and the integrity of the systems of governance in place for oversight. The financial sector is the most heavily regulated in all the history of capitalism. The simple reason is that it provides the core—it is the conductor, so to speak—of the diversity of effort and interests in the drive for wealth creation. But its equilibrium is fragile, resting as we indicated earlier on belief, that indefinable but well-known phenomenon—confidence.

Be that as it may, Jamaica's indigenous financial sector crash was, to date, one of the worst in the world, when measured as a percentage of Gross Domestic Product (GDP). It has been estimated by a World Bank review of forty-two banking crises to be third to Argentina's 1980 crisis, costing 55% of GDP, and Indonesia's 1997 crisis, costing 50% of GDP. Jamaica's cost was in the region of 44% of GDP.[62] Yet, as useful as it is in making comparisons possible, this method of assessing the cost of the crash fails to accurately establish both its immediate and long-term effects on the Jamaican economy and society.

To arrive at a more accurate estimate of cost, we must consider the allocative efficiency—or rather, inefficiency—of the credit boom in addition to the failure of the system to live up to the terms of loans represented by the boom. We must also review the negative repercussions on capital market development and the debilitating growth of government debt that directly resulted from the rehabilitation exercise. When all this is done and the prospects for growth in the Jamaican economy are considered, it will be understood that the crash of the indigenous financial services sector has left an enduring mark on the economy. It also has, to a great measure, established some strong constraints on the capacity of government to push for policies of growth in the near future.

The fact that the terms of loans granted during the boom were not fulfilled implies that additions to the capital stock were, from an economic efficiency standpoint, misallocated. Capital formation for the greater part of this period was therefore unproductive. Low or negative returns on the assets of these institutions make this obvious. Destruction of confidence of small savers and investors has also had harmful consequences that will require some time to remedy. Perhaps of greatest significance, however, is the inordinately large proportion of the assets in the financial system that are held by government as a result of its rescue operation—in the region of 45% of total deposits—and the fact that government debt represents close to 150% of GDP.

This state of affairs arises from conversion of FINSAC notes to government debt. In 2001 government took on its books the FINSAC notes issued to the banks and insurance companies. At that time, the value was $142.7 billion, or just over 40% of GDP. In September 2002, government also took over FINSAC's roughly $30 billion debt to the Bank of Jamaica. Because such a high proportion of banking system assets is government debt, and not credit to the private sector, risk is thereby reduced. However, maintaining restored confidence in the financial system will largely depend on the demonstrated ability of government to service this debt. This in turn requires government to achieve a growing primary surplus in the next few years.

However, if credit to the private sector for small businesses, mortgages, export production, and the like remains such a small proportion of the assets of the banking system, then the likelihood of expanded production and growth will be significantly reduced. Without growth, the tax base will not create the required primary surplus. Remedying this would require the imposition of new measures to either raise government revenues or lower government expenditures.

Undoubtedly FINSAC fulfilled the mandate given it by the government of Jamaica at its incorporation in January 1997. Resolution of the crisis avoided the worst scenarios of financial turmoil encountered elsewhere. It was also achieved in record time—one of the swiftest in the world so far—about six years.[63] But the cost has been heavy. There have been criticisms of the fact that a blanket guarantee was given to depositors, the insured, and pensioners. This was perhaps the costliest way to achieve the resolution. At the time, however, it was the way thought most feasible and acceptable to the population. There may have been alternatives that would have minimized costs, such as allowing depositors and other exposed clients of the system to bear some of the burden. Various schemes could be imagined and perhaps could have worked. There is no way of telling. In the heat and uncertainty generated by a crash, caution suggests going for known workable options. Seemingly, the art of the possible belongs not only to the realm of politics!

That there were only minor runs on two banks throughout the whole period of the meltdown must be seen as testimony to success in the objective of both protecting the insured, pensioners, and depositors and rehabilitating the financial sector. Proper legislation and governing institutions are now in place to make recurrence of this kind of crisis less likely. The legislation affecting banks, near-banks, building societies, industrial and provident societies, and deposit insurance schemes have all been passed (see Appendix D). There are stronger provisions for licensing banks, minimum levels of capitalization have been increased, and capital-to-deposit ratios have become more prudential. Lending to connected parties and overexposure in loan accommodation to any one borrower are now prohibited, and banking inspections have become more effective in uncovering transgressions. There is provision for greater scrutiny of persons acquiring control of financial institutions. Occurrences such as those associated with Blaise Trust and Merchant Bank and Century National Bank should not be as easy in the new environment.

Undoubtedly, the type of financial intermediation associated with the period we have referred to as euphoria contained all the classic elements associated with financial crises. Legislation and their attendant regulations can go a long way toward preventing crises—but like constitutions for countries, rules are interpreted and applied by people, with all their drives and foibles. If they are prudent, honest, intelligent, fair-minded, and willing to expend effort, things work well. This is a complex set of characteristics to find simultaneously embodied in one group of people, thus the unequivocal necessity for a system of checks and balances. Regardless of the existence of such systems, the world has never been able to rid itself of financial crises. No one could claim that Jamaica has eradicated the virus or bacterium that caused contagion and financial crisis. It seems, however, that it has moved a great distance on the path to making another meltdown, if not impossible, at least a bit less likely to happen again. The people who run the sector, however, will make the difference—they will have to demonstrate competence, integrity, and a willingness to recognize and tell the world when the "emperor has no clothes"! They will have to infuse in their quest to win, a moral element that attenuates greed, a wisdom that trumps street smarts, and a longer-term view that emphasizes strategy as opposed to immediate but merely tactical and apparent financial gain. Whether this is achievable shall be determined only as time passes.

Endnotes

1. Faculty at the UWI are allowed to do paid consultations in their field. This is useful from several perspectives. It usually involves some level of research and therefore creation of new knowledge—at least for the individual if not in a general sense. This material can then be used either in further research or to enhance teaching. Pardon a tidbit I feel compelled to share with readers. Early in my tenure at the University, Sir Allen Lewis, who was later to become our Chancellor, had written of the "psychic" income academics derived from their work at UWI. He was commenting on a dispute between the West Indies Group of University Teachers [WIGUT] and the University over wages. Consultations provided a bit of real as opposed to 'psychic' income!

2. Borrowed from epidemiology, contagion refers to "disease transmitted by direct or indirect contact." In financial services terms, it occurs when problems of declining confidence and/or insolvency spread across institutions directly, if they are linked in a conglomerate, or indirectly, in the case of institutions with unconnected ownership or management structures—author's footnote.

3. This terse but appropriate description of Jamaica's 1996 indigenous financial sector crash is to be found in Bank of Jamaica's historical account of its first forty years: "Bank of Jamaica: The First 40 Years." p.162.

4. Lue Lim, 1991.

5. Bank of Jamaica: *"Bank of Jamaica—The First 40 Years 1961–2000,"* p.4.

6. An informal savings scheme in which a 'banker' is chosen from among a group which pledges to save periodically, a specific sum of money. Each member of the 'partner' is guaranteed a draw of the total sum. Priority on the 'draw' is determined initially by lot.

7. Commercial banks issued currency notes in Jamaica until imposition of the Currency Notes Law of 1939 when this right was withdrawn. The right of Barclays Bank DCO to issue notes however, could not be withdrawn—having arisen from a Royal Charter that could not be abrogated by inferior colonial legislation.

8. The term "Group" generally referred to a collection of legal entities controlled by one individual or set of principals. The "Group" was never necessarily a collection of vibrantly functioning operations. It sometimes consisted of paper companies formed with an eye to the future—in most cases a speculative future of growth and profits—as well as with an eye to tax avoidance and regulatory arbitrage. The notion of the 'goodness' of the group structure had so invaded the mindset of the Jamaican entrepreneurial class during this period, that even in creating a private school it was thought fit to include the word "Group" in its title!

9. Financial services provided approximately 4% of GDP in 1975. By 1987 its value was 7% and by 1994 it reached a high of 16%—STATIN, Statistical Yearbook and Statistical Review; Planning Institute of Jamaica [PIOJ]: *Economic and Social Survey Jamaica*, various issues.

10. Hausmann and Fernandez-Arias, p.

11. Morris, [1999] page 7.

12. Auletta, [1986] pp. 30–31.

13. Ibid. p. 44.

14. Galbraith, [1997] page xii, emphasis added.

15. Ibid. p. xi

16. Chen-Young, p.9.

17. In an interview Hugh Small, former Minister of Finance, Government of Jamaica, was emphatic on this goal of the Multilaterals in their discussions and negotiations with Jamaica.

18. Bonnick, 1998, p.5.

19. Ibid. p.5.

20. Chen-Young, 1998, p.5.

21. Ibid. p. 5.

22. Lowenstein, page 130.

23. The former Chairman and CEO of Island Life Insurance Company in an interview with the author, admits to the fact that competitors stole Island Life's top performing agents. Competitors' showcase Head Offices and generous compensation packages lead to a migration of agents which in his view Island Life had to stem. He argues that the general feeling was that his company was losing ground and would be destroyed by the competition. To the author's suggestion, both prior to and after the crash, that had he not gone for the edifice, his company could have become the major player in the life insurance industry, he responded by justifying the decision on the ground of competitive response. On the issue of colour and class see for instance the works of Henriques and Braithwaite referenced in the bibliography.

24. Auletta, 1986 pp. 223–225.

25. Sometime prior to eventual sale of Lehman to Shearson/American Express, "…*ConAgra…[one of Lehman's]…regular clients, a large agriculture and food company based in Omaha, Nebraska, was prepared to pay $600 million to acquire Lehman. This was more than three times Lehman's worth at the time.*" [Auletta, 1986. p. 153] This offer was concealed from the partners and Board of Directors by one of the Co-CEOs. The offer was more than $200 million more than the purchase price for which Lehman finally settled. Although the partners did not lose on that transaction, they would have been much better off had the former deal been done.

26. Lump-sum interest-sensitive policies are marked by minimal life insurance coverage and a large investment input. Primarily investment vehicles, they were funded usually by a single lump-sum deposit. Interest paid on these policies was unrelated to the performance of any investment. The link to insurance came through a small amount of the deposit going into insurance coverage. In many cases the actuarial valuation of the insurance component was worth less than 1% of the investment component. For example, in the case of Mutual Life, of a total lump-sum portfolio liability of approximately

$2.1B only $168M or .08% went to insurance coverage for its 6,513 lump-sum policyholders. In more than 90% of lump-sum interest-sensitive policies, the policyholder's life was insured for $60,000 or less compared to average coverage of approximately $250,000 in the savings-type interest sensitive policies.

27. Galbraith, *The Great Crash 1929*, p.170.

28. Island Victoria Bank paid interest on checking accounts; it also competed on price [interest rates] against the big banks for large corporate deposits. To offset these costs its Board then exhorted loan officers to build a portfolio rapidly [interview with Oliver Jones]. In personal conversation, Jamaica's Minister of Finance recounts a comment made to him as he expressed his concern about the fact that funds would have to be found to payout depositors in Century National Bank. The response was "*What deposits, I didn't think people put money in that bank. I thought you only borrowed from Century.*" He insists it was not anecdotal!

29. The source of this list is various studies undertaken by and for FINSAC with a view to limiting the impact of the crisis; www.finsac.com.

30. Interview with Patrick Hylton.

31. This principal appears to have been a retired American businessman managing available investible funds. With Jamaica strapped for foreign exchange in the 1970s and early 1980s, this was a rather profitable and secure outlet for these funds. These transactions involved a sovereign Government that had so far never defaulted on a loan commitment. Connections to Jamaica previously included advances of funds for import purchases of the State owned entities—Forest Industries Development Company (FIDCO), the Jamaica Public Service Company (Jamaica's then State-owned electricity generating company) and the Water Commission—the state's provider of water to Jamaica. Interest rates on these transactions were generally in excess of 20%. [Patrick Hylton Interview].

32. House of Parliament: "Statement by the Minister of Finance summarizing the major points concerning the Blaise Financial Institutions", May 16, 1995, page 2. Emphases added.

33. Ibid. p.8, emphasis added.

34. Blaise Building Society, Inspectors Report October 1995, p. 55.

35. Offices of the Prime Minister.

36. Affidavit of Omar Davies Suit No. M 71 of 1996.

37. Omar Davies Affidavit Suit No. M 71 of 1996.

38. In financial crisis resolution the concept "good bank, bad bank" refers to the procedure of removing non-performing assets—usually loans—from the institution's balance sheet in order to restore it to solvency.

39. Jamaica Daily Gleaner August 2, 2001, page 1.

40. New York Times, July 1, 2005.

41. Ibid.

42. Eichenwald, Kurt, "*Conspiracy of Fools*", pp. 342–343.

43. Ibid. page 379.

44. Ibid. page1.

45. Ibid. page 1.

46. Interview with Minister Davies.

47. Bonnick, 1998, p. 7.

48. Morris, p. 81–103, offers a lively and interesting discussion.

49. Interview with Shirley Tyndal.

50. Daisy Coke, a Jamaican Actuary, chaired a Commission established to consider the degree of independence the Bank of Jamaica should enjoy. Bonnick's minority report argued for a greater measure of independence and tighter controls over funding to government from the Central Bank.

51. Chairman's remarks, FINSAC Annual Report, 1998.

52. FINSAC Annual Report, 1998.

53. FINSAC Annual Report 1998.

54. FINSAC Notes were promises to pay, promissory notes issued by FINSAC with the guarantee of the Government of Jamaica. These notes would be viewed as financial paper, securities of known base value with a known formula for determining interest earned and payment procedure. Effectively, FINSAC was, on behalf of the government, creating money though not in liquid form in immediate circulation.

55. This Requirement for a 26.5% holding of an intervened company's ordinary shares was legally necessary to preserve FINSAC's right to challenge any action of the majority shareholders deemed to prejudice the 'work-out plan' agreed as a condition precedent to FINSAC support. Peripherally, it also would provide lower cost funds as well as transfer part of the risk to the taxpayer—risk both of gain and loss.

56. Source: FINSAC: www.finsac.com.

57. The building ended up in the hands of the American Embassy at a price well below its construction cost. Neighbourhood residents, concerned about the number of touts, vendors, and others who would flock to the area protested use of the property as an Embassy. It is now proposed as a residence for the Embassy's employees.

58. This required the Minister of Finance to approve a 'scheme of arrangement' and issue a Vesting Order, merging the assets and business of the four banks under the Citizens Bank license, as provided for under the Banking Act.

59. The source material for this section is www.finsac.com.

60. Statement to Parliament, May 19, 1999, by Hon. Omar Davies, Minister of Finance.

61. Former Governor of the Bank of Jamaica, Jacques Buissieres, in a speech to the Life Insurance Companies Association of Jamaica, March 8, 1996. Reported in the Jamaica Observer, March 18, 1996. Emphases added.

62. World Bank Country Study—The Road to Sustained Growth in Jamaica, Figure 4.1: Fiscal Costs of Banking Crisis, p.88.

63. At the end of 2002 FINSAC's operations were essentially completed. The winding up of remaining activities is being handled by FIS with direction from the Ministry of Finance.

APPENDIX A

Commercial Banks in Jamaica, 1836–2002

Year	Banks	Branches/Agencies
1836	1	—
1846	3	18
1946	4	25
1960	6	65
1975	9	179
1979	8	150
1986	10	155
1990	11	170
1993	12	173

Year of Establishment	Commercial Bank
1836	Bank of Jamaica (not same as Central Bank)
1837	Colonial Bank
1839	Planters Bank
1864	London and Colonial Bank (merged with Barclays, 1925)
1889	Bank of Nova Scotia (local incorporation, 1966)
1911	Royal Bank of Canada
1920	Canadian Imperial Bank of Commerce
1925	Barclays Bank (merged with London & Colonial Bank)
1926	Bank of the British West Indies
1927	Canadian Bank Indies Limited (Sterling Bank)
1959	Bank of London and Montreal

Year of Establishment	*Commercial Bank*
1959	Bank of Surrey (became Bank of London and Montreal, 1970)
1960	First National City Bank (now Citibank)
1967	Jamaica Citizens Bank (Citizens and Southern Bank)
1971	First National Bank of Chicago
1973	Workers Savings and Loan Bank
1977	National Commercial Bank (former Barclays Bank)
1981	First Jamaica National Bank (purchase of First National Bank of Chicago)
1982	Bank of Credit and Commerce Int'l Ltd.
1984	Girod Bank (renamed Century National Bank, 1986)
1988	Eagle Commercial Bank
1993	Island Victoria Bank

*   Source: Lue Lim, BOJ

APPENDIX B

Structure of Jamaican Financial System, 1994–1996

*

	($ Million; % of Total)		
	1994	*1995*	*1996*
Assets of Financial Institutions			
1. Central Bank	66,468; 28.5	74,188; 26.3	76,064; 23.8
2. Commercial Banks	65,616; 28.2	89,544; 31.7	101,949; 32.0
3. Merchant Banks	14,837; 6.4	17,334; 6.1	23,262; 7.3
4. Building Societies	26,252; 11.3	29,059; 10.3	32,962; 10.3
5. Credit Unions	2,708; 1.2	4,098; 1.5	5,833; 1.8
6. Finance Houses & Trust Co.	746; 0.3	639; 0.2	566; 0.2
Deposit-Taking Institutions	110,159; 47.3	140,674; 49.9	164,572; 51.6
7. Development Banks	5,590; 2.4	7,712; 2.7	9,352; 2.9
8. Insurance Companies			
a. Life Insurance	28,810; 12.4	33,939; 12.0	36,555; 11.5
b. General Insurance	7,500; 3.2	8,753; 3.1	9,946; 3.1
c. Pension Funds Managed by Insurance Companies	10,455; 4.5	12,726; 4.5	16,980; 5.3
9. National Insurance Fund	3,850; 1.7	4,161; 1.5	5,568; 1.7
Total Assets of Financial Institutions (TAFI)	232,832; 100	282,153; 100	319,037; 100
Securities			
1. Stock Market Capitalization	48,700; 53.1	50,764; 49.4	66,116; 48.4
2. Government Securities	42,981; 46.9	51,988; 50.6	70,577; 51.6

(Continued)[*]

($ Million; % of Total)

	1994	1995	1996
Total Securities	91,681; 100	102,752; 100	136,693; 100
Gross Domestic Product (GDP)	129,310; 100	165,284; 100	202,138; 100
TAFI/GDP in %	180.1	170.7	157.8
Securities/GDP in %	70.9	62.2	67.6

[*]   Source: Building a Healthy Financial System for Jamaica's Future, Report to FINSAC; D. C. Cole; B. F. Slade; and T. E. Power, August 1997.

APPENDIX C

Companies Acquired by FIS/
FINSAC Following
Intervention

*

Group	Number	Cumulative Total
Blaise		
Blaise Building Society		
Blaise Investments Ltd.		
Blaise Trust and Merchant Bank Ltd.		
Consolidated Holdings Ltd.	4	4
Caldon		
Caldon Finance Group Ltd.		
Caldon Finance Merchant Bank Ltd.	2	6
Century National		
CNB Holdings		
Century National Building Society		
Century National Bank Ltd.		
Century National Merchant Bank & Trust Co, Ltd.		
Century National Developments Ltd.	5	11
Life of Jamaica/Citizens		
Atlantic Southern Insurance Company Ltd.		
Global Bahamas Holdings Ltd.		
Global Life Assurance Bahamas Ltd.		
Global Life Assurance Company Ltd.		

(Continued)[*]

Group	Number	Cumulative Total
Hitek Software Engineers Ltd.		
Lested Development Company Ltd.		
Life of Jamaica Ltd.		
LOJ Property Management Ltd.		
Citizens Asset Management Ltd.		
Citizens Bank (Guyana) Ltd.		
Citizens Bank Jamaica Ltd.		
Citizens Building Society		
Citizens Fla & Insurance Agency		
Citizens Merchant Bank Ltd.		
Doncaster Holdings Ltd.		
Ifcol Leasing Ltd.		
Jamaica Citizens Investment Ltd.		
Odessa Services Ltd.		
World Trade Services Corporation	19	30

Corporate (Workers Bank)

Corporate Group Ltd.		
Ardenne Ltd.		
Cabs Investments Ltd.		
Capital Assurance Building Society		
CMB Investments Ltd.		
Consumer Brands Ltd.		
Continental Import/Export Ltd.		
Corporate Insurance Brokers Ltd.		
Corporate Life Insurance Company Ltd.		
Corporate Merchant Bank Ltd.		

(Continued)[*]

Group	Number	Cumulative Total
CMB Investments Ltd.		
Formidable Ltd.		
Friends Group Ltd.		
Hambro Holdings Ltd.		
Island Broadcasting Services Ltd.		
Negril Investments Ltd.		
Negril Holdings Ltd.		
Workers Bank Capital and Finance Ltd. (UK)		
Workers Bank Finance Investments Ltd.		
Workers Savings and Loan Bank	20	50
Dyoll		
Dyol Group Ltd.		
Buck Securities Partners Ltd.		
Buck Management Ltd.		
Buck Securities Merchant Bank Ltd.		
Buck Security Brokers Ltd.		
Buck Ventures Ltd.		
Caribbean National Group Ltd.		
Cayman Financial Services		
Cayman Insurance Centre		
Dyoll Caribbean Financial Services Ltd.		
Dyoll Insurance Company Ltd.		
Dyoll Life Insurance Company Ltd.		
Dyoll/Wataru Coffee Co. Ltd.		
National Building Society of Cayman Ltd.		
New Seville Development Ltd.	15	65

(Continued)[*]

Group	Number	Cumulative Total
Eagle		
Billy Dunn Development Co. Ltd.		
Ciboney Group Ltd.		
Ciboney Apartments Ltd.		
Ciboney Caribbean Resorts Ltd.		
Ciboney Colony Management Ltd.		
Ciboney Holdings Ltd.		
Ciboney Hotel Developers Ltd.		
Ciboney Hotels Ltd.		
Ciboney Investments Ltd.		
Ciboney Ocho Rios Ltd.		
Ciboney Proprietors Ltd.		
Country Inns By LRI		
Leisure Operators Ltd.		
Luxury Resorts Enterprises Ltd.		
Luxury Resorts International Ltd.		
Number Sixty Ltd.		
Radisson Ciboney All Inclusive Resorts Ltd.		
Cinchona Heights Ltd.		
Coolit Ltd.		
Crown Eagle Hotels Ltd.		
Crown Eagle Life Insurance Co. Ltd.		
Crowne Plaza Holdings Ltd.		
DARU Investment Ltd.		
Dent-Plan Ltd.		
Eagle Commercial Bank Ltd.		

(Continued)*

Group	Number	Cumulative Total
Eagle Foundation for Enterprise		
Eagle General Insurance Co. Ltd.		
Eagle Holdings and Investments Ltd.		
Eagle Holdings (Cayman) Ltd.		
Eagle Housing Development Corporation Ltd.		
Eagle I.R.P. Ltd.		
Eagle Information Systems Ltd.		
Eagle Insurance Brokers Ltd.		
Eagle Insurance Company (Cayman) Ltd.		
Eagle Merchant Bank (Cayman) Ltd.		
Eagle Merchant Bank (Jamaica) Ltd.		
Eagle Nominees Ltd.		
Eagle Permanent Building Society		
Eagle Premium Growth Fund		
Eagle Trade Services Ltd.		
Eagle Trust Company Ltd.		
Eagle Unit Trusts Management Co. Ltd.		
Ebony View Ltd.		
Exeter Holdings Ltd.		
Fairfield Development Ltd.		
First Capital Advisory Corporation		
First Equity Corporation of Florida		
Flexnon Ltd.		
Forte Belle Management Company Ltd.		
Hill Haven Ltd.		
Hospitality Inns of Jamaica Ltd.		

(Continued)[*]

Group	Number	Cumulative Total
Innswood Distilleries Ltd.		
Jamaica Fruit & Shipping Ltd.		
Martins Coach & Cars Ltd.		
Martins Travel Service Ltd.		
Oakville Ltd.		
Old England Coffee Development Co. Ltd.		
Optima Investment Management Ltd.		
Paul Chen-Young and Associates Ltd.		
Peninsular Ltd.		
Pier 1 Development Company Ltd.		
Sunset Island Resorts Ltd.		
Top Rated Holdings Ltd.		
Westcoast Holdings Ltd.		
Woodpecker Ltd.	65	130
Horizon		
Horizon Group Ltd.		
CPMS		
Dolphin Distributors Ltd.		
Horizon Building Society		
Horizon Consulting Services Ltd.		
Horizon Development Company Ltd.		
Horizon Financial Services Ltd.		
Horizon Insurance Brokers Ltd.		
Horizon Life Insurance Ltd.		
Horizon Merchant Bank Ltd.		
Horizon Securities Ltd.		

(Continued)[*]

Group	Number	Cumulative Total
Horizon Trade Services Ltd.		
Kemicals Worldwide Ltd.		
Sun Investments & Finance		
Swift Chemicals Ltd.	15	145
Island Life		
Cherry Gardens Homes Ltd.		
Island Life Insurance Company Ltd.		
Island Life Merchant Bank Ltd.		
Island Resource Ltd.		
Island Victoria Bank Ltd.		
(Jointly with Victoria Mutual)	5	150
Mutual Life		
Jamaica Mutual Life Assurance Company Ltd.		
866 Realty Inc.		
Bloody Bay Hotel Development Ltd.		
Commercial & Residential Development Ltd.		
Dural Investments Ltd.		
Halsbury Ltd.		
International Hotels (Overseas) Ltd.		
International Hotels (St. Lucia) Ltd.		
International Hotels Ltd.		
Jamaica Hotel Properties Associates Ltd.		
Jamaica Hotels Ltd.		
Jamaica Housing Ltd.		
Jamaica M & N Investments Ltd.		
Jamaica Mutual Inc.		

(Continued)*

Group	Number	Cumulative Total
Jamaica Mutual Pension Fund		
Jamaica Mutual Properties Ltd.		
Mutual Services Caribbean Ltd.		
N.E.M. Insurance Co. Ltd.		
Restaurant Associates Ltd.	19	169

NCB

National Commercial Bank Group Ltd.

Caribbean Home N.C.B. Insurance Company Ltd.

CARP Corporation Ltd.

Cherry Brook Ltd.

Club Jamaica Beach Resort Ltd.

Computer Services and Programming Ltd.

Data Cap Processing Ltd.

Edward Gayle and Company Ltd.

EPSOM Holdings Ltd.

Glen Abbey Ltd.

Jamaica Orange Company Ltd.

Mammee Bay Resorts Ltd.

Mutual Securities Ltd.

Mutual Security Insurance Brokers Ltd.

N.C.B. Hotels Ltd.

N.C.B. Insurance Services Ltd.

N.C.B. Investments Ltd.

N.C.B. Jamaica Cayman Ltd.

N.C.B. Jamaica (Nominees) Ltd.

N.C.B. Trust & Merchant Bank Ltd.

(Continued)*

Group	Number	Cumulative Total
National Commercial Bank (Jamaica) Ltd.		
National Mutual Investments Ltd.		
Noxio Ltd.		
Pembroke Hotel Enterprises Ltd.		
Securicor (Jamaica) Ltd.		
West Indies Trust Company Ltd.	26	195
Non-Groups		
Fidelity Finance Merchant Bank Ltd.		
Fidelity Investments Ltd.	2	197
Billy Craig Finance Merchant Bank Ltd.	1	198
Intercontinental Merchant Bank Ltd.	1	199
Partner Merchant Bank Ltd.	1	200

*   *In most cases, these acquisitions were 100%
Source: FINSAC Annual Reports and Organization Charts

APPENDIX D

Relevant Remedial Legislation Affecting the Financial Services Sector

·

1992, December 9—The Banking Act

This act resulted in the creation of a totally new act for commercial banks. Its most significant provisions were:

1. Stronger provisions regarding licensing, minimum levels of capital and levels of deposits which could be taken;

2. Stricter prudential controls on the activities of institutions, such as insider loans, investments in commercial companies and levels of lending to single customers or to groups;

3. Provisions for possible loan losses;

4. Greater scrutiny of persons acquiring control of institutions;

5. Strengthening of the powers of the supervisors, both of the inspection department and the Minister;

6. Enhancement of regulation-making powers to achieve greater flexibility in areas such as the adequacy of capital, solvency, the obtaining of cooperation and the maintenance of high personal standards among persons working in the banking industry; and

7. A full and comprehensive mechanism for identifying and dealing with offences of and troubled conditions relating to institutions including ways of rescuing troubled institutions.

1992, December 31—The Financial Institutions Act

This act replaced the Protection of Depositors Act (PDA):

It essentially provided regulations for those "near banks" which take deposits from the public. The provisions in this act were similar to those of the Banking Act of 1992, save that the financial institutions were not permitted to operate checking accounts.

(Continued)[*]

1994, December 19—The Bank of Jamaica (Specified Financial Institutions) (Industrial and Provident Societies) Act 1994

Designation of these [Industrial and Provident] societies as "Specified Financial Institutions" gave the Bank of Jamaica the power to supervise and examine them.

1994, December 31—The Bank of Jamaica (Specified Financial Institutions) (Building Societies) Act 1994

The designation of building societies as "Specified Financial Institutions" gave the power to supervise and examine them.

1997, October 29—The Banking Act and The Financial Institutions Act

1997, December 10—The Building Societies Act

These were amendments to the previous acts designed to achieve the following:

1. To improve the machinery for regulation and supervision of commercial banks, licensed financial institutions and building societies; and

2. To empower the regulatory authorities to take decisive action to bring about restructuring of any of these institutions which cease to be viable.

1997, December 10—The Industrial and Provident Societies Act

The purpose of this amendment was to prevent unregulated and unsupervised entities, which were registered under the Industrial and Provident Societies Act from taking deposits from the public without expressed authorisation from the Minister of Finance.

1998, August 31—The Deposit Insurance Act 1998

The act established the Deposit Insurance Scheme, which is operated by the Jamaica Deposit Insurance Corporation. The scheme was designed to cover specified deposits held with commercial banks, financial institutions licensed under the Financial Institutions Act, building societies and institutions whose business includes the taking of deposits and who have been designated by the Minister of Finance as "Specified Financial Institutions" pursuant to the Bank of Jamaica Act.

[*]   Source: *Bank of Jamaica: The First 40 Years 1961–2000*, Bank of Jamaica, 2004.

APPENDIX E

FINSAC Intervention Costs to Year 2002

*

Institution	Cash	FINSAC Paper	Total
Billy Craig Merchant Bank		148,018	148,018
Buck & Caribbean Trust		62,679	62,679
Caldon Merchant Bank		121,739	121,739
Citizens Bank		2,767,160	2,767,160
Eagle Group	3,534,854	14,514,988	18,049,842
Dyoll Group	456,382	509,481	965,863
Fidelity Merchant Bank		89,142	89,142
Horizon Group	34,730	5,507,541	5,542,271
Island Life Insurance Company	969,948	787,150	1,757,098
Intercontinental Merchant Bank Ltd.		100,384	100,384
Jamaica Mutual Life Insurance Society	5,622,744	11,075,268	16,698,012
Life of Jamaica	988,347	3,909,359	4,897,706
NCB Group		20,899,698	20,899,698
Victoria Mutual Building Society		1,717,658	1,717,658
Union Bank of Jamaica	2,300,000	6,473,666	8,773,666
Corporate Group/Workers Bank	2,030,429	9,535,303	11,565,732
Total Intervention Costs	**15,937,434**	**78,219,234**	**94,156,668**

* Intervention costs do not include interest associated with FINSAC paper, which is 1% above the weighted average Treasury bill rate and Bank of Jamaica overdraft.

APPENDIX F

Jamaica's Financial System: 1990, 1995, and 2001

*

	1990			1995			2001		
	No.	Assets	% Assets	No.	Assets	% Assets	No.[a]	Assets	% Assets
Com-mercial Banks	11	17,328	62.3	11	121,325	61.1	6	239,087	68.0
Non-Banks		10,469	37.7		77,271	38.9		112,745	32.0
Mer-chant Banks	21	4,527	16.3	25	17,334	8.7	13	15,632	4.4
Building Societ-ies	6	3,058	11.0	32	29,084	14.6	5	50,448	14.3
Credit Unions	80	812	2.9	82	4,098	2.1	66	17,279	4.9
Life Insur-ance Cos.	10	2,072	7.5	12	26,755	13.5	7	29,386[b]	8.4
Total Assets		27,797	100.0		198,596	100.0		351,832	100.0
% of GDP		86.5			100.6			100.8	

* Source: Bank of Jamaica, Life Insurance Company Association
  Notes: a. Number of institutions refers to 1999
        b. 2000

Bibliography

Akerly, George. "The Market for Lemons: Quality, Uncertainty and the Market Mechanism." *Quarterly Journal of Economics* 84 (August 1970): 488–500.

Auletta, Ken. *Greed and Glory on Wall Street: The Fall of the House of Lehman*, New York: Warner Books, 1986.

Bank of Jamaica. *Bank of Jamaica: The First 40 Years 1961–2000*, Kingston: Bank of Jamaica, 2004.

Bernstein, Peter, L. *Against the Gods: The Remarkable Story of Risk*, New York: John Wiley & Sons, 1996.

Bonnick, Gladstone. "Storm in a Teacup, or Crisis in Jamaica's Financial Sector." 14th Adlith Brown Memorial Lecture, Caribbean Centre for Monetary Studies, October 1998.

Balogh, Thomas. "The Effective Mobilization of Savings for Jamaican Development," a report to Minister of Finance N.N. Nethersole on implementation of the Towers Report.

Braithwaite, Lloyd. "Social Stratification in Trinidad: A Preliminary Analysis." *Social and Economic Studies* 2, no. 1 (June 1954).

Carron, Andrew, S. *The Plight of the Thrift Institutions*, Washington DC: Brookings Institution, 1982.

Chen-Young, Paul. "With All Good Intentions: The Collapse of Jamaica's Financial Sector." *Policy Papers on the Americas* 9, Study 12 (November, 1998).

Cipolla, Carlo. *Money, Prices and Civilization in the Mediterranean World: Fifth to Seventeenth Century*, N.J.: Princeton University Press, 1956.

Clarke, L., and D. Danns. *The Financial Evolution of the Caribbean Community: 1970–1996*, St. Augustine: Caribbean Centre for Monetary Studies, 1997.

Davies, Glyn. *A History of Money From Ancient Times to the Present Day*, Cardiff: University of Wales Press, 1994.

Davis, Gouzouli, Spence, and Star. "Measuring the Performance of Banks." *Business Strategy Review* 4, no. 3 (Autumn, 1993): 1–14.

Eichenwald, Kurt. *Conspiracy of Fools: A True Story*, New York: Broadway Books, 2005.

Friedman, Milton, and Anna Schwarz. *A Monetary History of the United States, 1867–1960*, Princeton: Princeton University Press, 1963.

Galbraith, J. K. *The Great Crash 1929*, Boston and New York: Houghton Mifflin Co., 1997.

Gertler, Mark. "Financial Structure and Aggregate Economic Activity: An Overview." *Journal of Money, Credit and Banking* 20 (August 2000): 559–588.

Hausmann, R, and E. Fernandez-Arias. *Foreign Direct Investment: Good Cholesterol?*, Working Paper No. 417, Inter-American Development Bank, Washington.

Henriques, F. *Family and Colour in Jamaica*, London: Macgibbon & Kee, 1968.

Kaminsky, Graciela, L. *Currency and Banking Crises: The Early Warnings of Distress*, Board of Governors of the Federal Reserve System, International Discussion Papers, Number 629, October, 1998.

Lee Kuan Yew. *From Third World to First: The Singapore Story: 1965–2000*, New York: Harper Collins, 2000.

Lowenstein, Roger. *When Genius Failed: The Rise and Fall of Long-Term Capital Management*, New York: Random House, 2000.

Lue Lim, Gail. *Jamaica's Financial System: Its Historical Development*, Kingston: Bank of Jamaica, 1991.

Malkiel, Burton. *A Random Walk Down Wall Street*, New York: W. W. Norton & Co., 1996.

McLean, Bethany, and Peter Elkind. *The Smartest Guys in the Room: The Amazing Rise and Scandalous Fall of ENRON*, Portfolio, Penguin Group (USA) Inc., 2004.

Mishkin, Frederic. *The Economics of Money, Banking and Financial Markets*, New York: Addison-Wesley, 1997.

Mishkin, Frederic. *Asymmetric Information and Financial Crises: A Historical Perspective*, in Hubbard, R. Glen (ed.): *Financial Markets and Financial Crises*, University of Chicago Press, Chicago & London, 1991, pp. 69–108.

Morris, Charles, R. *Money, Greed, and Risk: Why Financial Crises and Crashes Happen*, New York: Random House, 1999.

Salomon Brothers. *Cost Management in Global Banking: The Lessons of the Low Cost Producers*, Salomon Brothers, October 1993.

Spong, K., R. Sullivan, and R. DeYoung. *What Makes a Bank Efficient?—Look at Financial Characteristics and Bank Management and Ownership Structure*, Federal Reserve Bank of Kansas City.

Statistical Institute of Jamaica: *Statistical Yearbook of Jamaica*, various years.

Towers, Graham F. *The Financial System and Institutions of Jamaica*, 1956—Former Governor of the Bank of Canada through the United Nations Technical Assistance Administration.

Index

978-0-595-38534-8
0-595-38534-6

www.ingramcontent.com/pod-product-compliance
Lightning Source LLC
Chambersburg PA
CBHW030800180526
45163CB00003B/1100